An uncommon spiritual path

The quest to find Jesus beyond conventional Christianity

Dion A Forster

Other books by the same author

An introduction to Wesleyan Spirituality

A prayer guide for use during examinations

Christ at the centre – Discovering the Cosmic Christ
in the spirituality of Bede Griffiths

Copyright © 2008 by Dion A Forster

Published by:

AcadSA
P U B L I S H I N G

PO Box 12322
Edleen, Kempton Park
1625
Rep South Africa

Tel   +27 11 976-4044
Fax   +27 11 976-4042
email info@acadsa.co.za
web   www.acadsa.co.za

ISBN 978-1-920212-28-5

9 781920 212285

For my wife Megan,
my daughter Courtney,
and my son Liam.

In our life together
I discover the mystery of
God's love and grace.

Acknowledgements

This is my second book in less than a year. Such productivity comes at a price! There have been many late nights, early mornings, and stolen moments during the day as I have finalised the text for this book. I am grateful for the patience of my family, friends, and colleagues for allowing me the space and time to do this. This book had to be written! It resonates so strongly with my current desire to move beyond the 'trappings' of religion to the loving source of faith itself – Jesus Christ.

The contents of this book began to take shape over a decade ago. At that stage I had not yet discovered the wonderful work of Fr Bede Griffiths, which is so much closer to my own theology. However, at that stage my graduate supervisor, Professor Felicity Edwards, introduced me to the mind-bending spirituality of Abhishiktānanda. I knew then, as I know now, that a life committed to loving and knowing God takes great courage. It takes courage to break with convention. It takes courage to move out of what has become familiar and comfortable. It takes courage to go against the grain of conventional culture and religion. Abhishiktānanda's life and spirituality inspired me in all of these points! So, I am grateful to Felicity for patiently answering my questions about Christianity in relation to other living faiths and for helping me to understand some of the more subtle concepts of Indian philosophy and the Hindu religion. I am also grateful for those friends who had taken this journey before me, people like Dr Kevin Snyman, Rev David Newton, and Rev Rod Burton. Your courage inspired me to move ahead on my own unique spiritual journey.

Then there are those good friends who kept me grounded firmly within the richness of the spiritual traditions of my own context. They are the Revds George Marchinkowski, Christopher Judelsohn and Stephen van Schalkwyk. We had many long, often tense, theological conversations over tea, or at 'The Mot' in Grahamstown South Africa. Their ideas and insights helped to maintain the dynamic tension that informed my understanding of the possibility of being fully and wholly Christian without having to dismiss the work of God in other contexts and faiths.

I am an enthusiastic individual! This enthusiasm seems to reach its peak when I feel I have something new to share or teach. My colleagues in the Education for Ministry and Mission Unit of the Methodist Church of Southern Africa, and our seminary, John Wesley College, have blessed me with interest, affirmation, and celebration over the years. Professor Neville Richardson, Rev Madika Sibeko, and Rev Ruth Jonas are all fine scholars and even better friends! While I am mentioning friends and scholars, my friend Dr Wessel Bentley is a source of inspiration and motivation. Wessel and I have worked together on numerous academic projects. We seem to be a perfect team!

Each year the seminary sees a new batch of students for the ministry arrive. I have been part of the lives of 10 such groups since taking my first responsibility for ministerial formation in the Methodist Church (then still in Cape Town in the late 1990's). Each group has helped me to sharpen my thoughts, deepen my faith in God's Church, and learn new and exciting things about being a Christian in an African context. I thank God for their ministry and sacrifice to bring about Christ's 'healing and transformation' in society.

I have had many wonderful years serving at the Bryanston Methodist Church as an associate member of the clergy. I often feel guilty that I get to do what I love most, which is preach and teach, without having to worry about what really makes a Church function (meetings, budgets, pastoral concerns etc.) Thank you to all of the faithful members of the Church, and to the Revds Christopher Harrison, Janet Verrier, John Gillmer, Leon Klein, Mandla Gamede, Demetris Palos, Leon Klein, and Pastor Mark Russel.

This is the second book in this spirituality series. The first is entitled *Christ at the centre – Discovering the Cosmic Christ in the Spirituality of Bede Griffiths*. That book was dedicated to my parents. Sadly my father, Ian Forster, passed away just days before it was published. His death has reminded me to celebrate those whom I love, and to do so with urgency! It is for this reason that I have dedicated this book to my wife Megan, my daughter Courtney, and my son Liam. In our life together I have discovered God's gracious gift of life and love. Their lives complete mine.

By the time this book is published I shall be entering into a new phase of my life and ministry. In many ways this book reflects my own journey beyond the structures and symbols of the traditional Church. I am still deeply committed to the Methodist Church of Southern Africa. She is an instrument of God's salvation, justice, and mercy on our continent. I look forward to being under her discipline and in her service for many years to come. However, I do feel God calling me on a less common path. The future holds great promise, like Abhishiktānanda I am venturing into a new an uncertain territory. I am inspired and encouraged by his boldness to live with integrity and total devotion to Christ. I long for the same.

My friend, Graham Power, with whom I shall be working, has encouraged me to take time to pray, grow, make new discoveries, and write. I am grateful for the space that he is creating for me to do so. Please keep an eye on my website for future book projects.

Finally, I wish to thank Manfred Jung from AcadSA Publishing who has helped me to get my thoughts into print. He has spent hours on this project! I am amazed by his generosity and commitment! He is meticulous, careful, gracious, and works at an extraordinary pace! I am grateful for all that he has done on this book and the other books I have published through him.

ad maiorem dei gloriam

"For the greater glory of God"

Dr Dion Forster
John Wesley College, Pretoria (January 2008)
http://www.spirituality.org.za
dion@spirituality.org.za

Contents

Foreword

I have long held the conviction that people cannot be whole unless they have an active and deep spiritual life. One of the great shortcomings of many contemporary western cultures is that they lull us into believing that we can find peace, joy, and fulfilment in what we own, or in what we do. Sadly, many people have come to discover that the pursuit of wealth, power, and recognition by one's peers, are shallow and meaningless against the backdrop of what it means to be truly alive. When one considers that a human person has physical, psychological and spiritual needs, the pursuit of true and ultimate meaning becomes all the more important in a world that seems so increasingly devoid of depth.

This book charts a different course to the norm. It examines a way of life that may seem quite austere and strange to most of us. However, it will be shown that it is not the spiritual methodology, nor even the content of this particular spiritual path, that bring blessing and peace. Rather, it is passing beyond methods, ideas, and even doctrines, that brings us into the presence of the God who gives and sustains true life; the kind of life Jesus speaks of in John's Gospel (John 10:10).

My prayer is that you will approach this book with an open mind, and an open heart. As you read about the life and spirituality of Henri le Saux (commonly known as Abhishiktānanda – which means 'the bliss of Christ') consider what you could gain by moving beyond the trappings of religion, to the power of true faith itself. I am fairly certain that there may be some aspects of this spiritual approach, and its theological content, that will be unsettling to some – it is radical, and certainly not what most of us have come to associate with Christian spirituality, particularly not the kind of spirituality that is common in many sub-urban western churches.

Please don't give up on this journey, and on what you may discover, because of a theological or methodological difference. Moreover, I would encourage you not to get hung up with trying to fathom some of the more complex notions that arise from the interaction between Hindu and Christian philosophy and theology. As we shall discover, even these concepts will need to give way to the mystery of the God they seek to express, at some point.

The Pastor and theologian Brian Mclaren comments in one of his books that his grandmother told him that when you're eating fish you shouldn't worry too much about the bones, rather enjoy the meat, once that's done you can always come back and see if there is anything left that you want to reconsider or savour. Please treat this book in the same way. If you don't understand something at first, skip it! It probably doesn't matter much in the big scheme of things anyway! However, when you feel the need to go a little deeper come back to a paragraph, a phrase, or a concept in order to gain a fuller understanding of it.

At the end of the day my desire is not that you will come to think, or act, as Abhishiktānanda did. Nor is it that you will think or act as I do. Rather, my prayer for you is that you will have the courage to break through the pressure to conform to common expressions of Christian spirituality. Moreover, I pray that you will work with courage to quench your thirst for truth, and satisfy your hunger for God by charting a path that may not have been taken by any other person. That, in my opinion, is what makes Abhishiktānanda's spirituality so unique, valuable, and special. It is his courage to go against convention that makes him so worthy of study.

So, while his method and approach are suited to his particular context, his courage and desire to live for truth and discover God beyond the mere forms and symbols of religion are values that we can all share.

May you come to find that you, and all of creation, are contained within the Bliss of the Triune God.

Introduction - Threats and challenges in contemporary Christianity

Among the greatest threats upon contemporary Christianity are the influences of western individualism, materialism, and the loss of the sense of the spiritual and mystical in creation. The kind of Christianity that dominates popular culture often has more in common with a market driven sales mentality than it does with the Gospel of Jesus Christ. In a world where 'bigger' is regarded as 'better', where the success of a faith community is measured by the number of its adherents, and where programs and courses dominate the agenda for growth, there is a desperate need for some fresh, mature, and deep expressions of faith.

My own personal experience has borne out that shallow expressions of faith, such as those mentioned above, are not sufficient to meet the profound and real needs of truly spiritual people. Within them there is little to sustain the soul, transform the individual, and bring true and lasting meaning in an often harsh and demanding world. It is little wonder that so many young people are turning away from 'structured' religion towards post-modern expressions of spirituality and faith. Sadly, in their pursuit for true meaning, many have lost the great depths and truths – such as the revelation of God, and the salvation of Christ – that come from a sincere, lived, relationship with God in Christ.

I believe that an expression of faith that is free from the symbolic and linguistic constraints of moral and religious fundamentalism is at the very centre of the Gospel of Christ. It is for life that Jesus came (John 10:10), and this life is to be found in the mystery of the one who IS life.

A reaction among more conservative Christians to this shift in spiritual interest, particularly as it relates to the religions of the East, has been to demonise and undermine the revelatory and spiritual value that Christians can gain from the practises, and devotion, of these other faiths. Let us never assume that God was not active, both in revelation and salvation, before there was a Church, or doctrines, or even the Christian scriptures themselves. God is alive, and has always infused all life with God's presence. I am saddened when I hear people speaking about the 'threat' of this religion or that one. There seems to be a very unhealthy disregard for the fact that God loves all people, and that God reveals God's self equally and graciously to all who seek. The sad assumption for many is that God is uniquely 'Christian', and particularly that God is a European or American Christian. This is ludicrous. God is God! We may be Christian, and our context may be that of America or Europe, but surely we acknowledge that God is so much more than these things? God is not contained completely within religion, rather religion is an attempt to contain aspects and approaches to God in order to move beyond these elements in pursuit of the truth of the God who is life itself.

What is required is thus a recapturing of the depth and wisdom of mystical spirituality from the varied sources of God's revelation. This should be a spirituality that will meet the deep longing and need for people to discover and live within the truth of an almighty God who is living and active in all spheres of life. There is a need to discover that God is greater than the mere doctrines, symbols, or expressions, of any one faith. Whilst these elements of religion are not to be discarded, since they have value, they must be transcended in order to move into the mystery of the True God who cannot be contained in words and concepts.

Many are afraid of surpassing what is safe. I share some of those fears. Dealing with what is known does bring a sense of comfort and ease. However, the misunderstanding that seems to operate in much of contemporary religion is that if one passes beyond something it must be rejected. So, if I move beyond a particular way of worshipping God, or reading the Bible, or being in community, I have 'outgrown' it and so should no longer accept it as having any value. This view is not consistent or compatible with the central tenets of the Gospel, a Gospel of grace, inclusion, love, and acceptance of the 'other' – Peter Storey speaks of this Gospel value as being a 'radical hospitality'.

An analogy of how one should integrate what one has moved beyond can be found in the relationship between the letters of the alphabet, and stories that are written in books. A letter is an essential element of a word. Without letters, words cannot exist. Words are dependent upon letters for their 'existence'. So, we can say that letters have a measure of value and meaning. However, it also needs to be said that letters by themselves have a much less complete value and meaning than the words they are used to form – letters gain greater value and meaning when they are put together to form words. Words, too, are meaningful by themselves, yet when they are put into sentences their value and meaning increases. The same can be said for sentences as they become paragraphs, paragraphs as they become chapters in a book, and chapters as they make up a story.

Each part is necessary within the whole. None is less or more valuable in terms of the whole, since each is interdependent upon the others for its value and meaning. However, when the lower level elements are integrated into higher and more complex structures the value of the whole unit is deepened and increased. This same principle relates to our faith. As we grow through life and seek deeper and more significant truth, we should integrate those experiences, symbols, and truths we have surpassed. In doing so we bring a far greater meaning and depth to the whole of our lives. It would not only be a mistake, but in fact untrue, to deny who we once were and simply live as if we are only the persons we are at this moment in time. My present state of being has been fundamentally shaped by my past. Sometimes it has been shaped by positive choices, beliefs and practices, and at other times by what I have learned from mistakes, falsehoods, and pain. Present identity is a complex phenomenon.

It is just such a 'complex' and 'integrative' journey that this book considers. This is a journey to the further shore, a journey of discovery, a journey that charts new territories in pursuit of the God who cannot be contained entirely within one religion, one theology, or even one spirituality.

This book considers the quest of a remarkable French Monk, and offers some insights into his spiritual journey, guiding us to note what we can learn from it in our own quest for a truly faithful and significant Christian spirituality. The book considers how this monk, Henri le Saux (most commonly known by the name he adopted in India, Abhishiktānanda, which means 'the bliss of Christ'), rediscovered the mystery and life of the triune God through the culture and religion of India. He travelled to the 'further shore', by becoming a Hindu

sanyassi[1], adopting their dress, manner, and lifestyle, and in doing so he discovered a new life in God that was more than a mere adherence to a religion or a practise of spirituality. I would argue that he became a true Christ follower, a courageous disciple of Jesus, by surpassing conventional Christianity. This was a bold and courageous move!

Experience tells me that we cling to the familiarity of our religion, not necessarily because it is the whole 'truth' (in the sense of being the only truth there is within the universe), but rather because it has become 'a truth' for us. What makes this truth so powerful is that it is grounded within our experience. It has been shaped by who we are, by our relationship with God, and our relationship with the rest of God's creation. This is not entirely bad. However, there is an unhealthy reliance on the *self* in this kind of approach to faith. Surely truth is about more than just what has become true for me? What is true for me needs to be transcended as I discover greater and more complex truths, until eventually I discover truth itself in the mystery of God – the God who is 'truth'. He writes of this new life,

> The wandering Indian *sannyasi* is indeed very similar to the itinerant messenger of the Gospel ... he is free from all anxiety and preoccupation, being without ties of any kind, whether to things, places or people. Wherever he goes he is a stranger, and yet everywhere he is at home, since he is sovereignly free in his absolute renunciation ... For he knows well that it is only by fleeing far away from everything, and in the first place from himself, by passing beyond everything, and above all beyond himself, that man can attain to God, the Unattainable. (Abhishiktānanda 1990:9).

The first part of this book will consider how Swāmi[2] Abhishiktānanda's life and spirituality can be characterised by his quest to constantly move 'beyond' in order to attain the Unattainable. Although his initial desire was to remain fundamentally Christian in India, his quest for the Absolute led him to move beyond the accepted norms of both Christianity and

---

1   A *sanyassi* is person who has devoted his life to the spiritual quest of discovering and living the mystery of God. In the Hindu religion a *sanyassi* normally devotes himself to extended periods of meditation and prayer, surviving by begging for 'alms' from others. Perhaps the closest equivalent in Christianity would be a wondering monk.

2   The title Swāmi refers to a spiritual teacher or guide.

Hinduism. This was no easy journey, he encountered a great deal of inner turmoil in this process. His struggle was between his experience of Upanishadic *advaita*, and his loyalty to the commonly accepted understanding of what it means to faithfully follow Christ. This complex inner turmoil can be largely evidenced in his external struggle between the trappings of western monasticism, and the life of a wandering Indian *sannyāsi*. His interior and exterior struggle, which were both parts of a single reality, shaped and formed his whole life, his ministry, and so too his faith. As we shall see the inner life, and the outer life, are inextricably linked in the development of Abhishiktānanda's non-dual spirituality. In this book we shall come to discover that his life was a courageous journey of faith that often required him to break new ground in his quest to discover a true mystical experience of God.

The next section of this book will trace that journey, by focussing on the life and experience of Abhishiktānanda. The book will also discuss and evaluate the growth and development of what, on the surface, may seem to be a contradictory concept; that is, Abhishiktānanda's Christian advaitic spirituality – often called a Hindu-Christian spirituality.

In the sections that follow, attention will be given to the theological concepts that underlie his spirituality, as well as presenting and evaluating the theology that resulted from his spiritual journey. Finally, the book will present the contribution, challenges, and opportunities that arise from Swāmi Abhishiktānanda's advaitin spirituality.

Once again, I would encourage you to approach this book with an open heart and mind. I have personally moved beyond some of the concepts and ideas that I will write about below. However, they do form a significant part of my present spiritual experience and identity. So, while my theology may have changed and adapted in recent years, the one thing that remains unchanged is my admiration for the courageous manner in which Abhishiktānanda devoted himself to discovering and loving God. That courage took him on an uncommon spiritual path. His path may differ from mine, or yours, yet I hope that we shall have the courage and devotion to strive for the same goal – absolute loving commitment to the Triune God.

There is so much to be learned from the courage and commitment of this remarkable spiritual pilgrim. I pray that you will find some value and insight from Abhishiktānanda's journey that will enliven and enrich your own.

Context and courage – the shaping of an unconventional spirituality.

Something that should become clear in this section is the courage with which Abhishiktānanda sought to address the context in which his faith developed, and the courage that it took to take an uncharted path.

It bears keeping in mind that Abhishiktānanda's path is not for every spiritual seeker. However, the manner in which he devoted himself with integrity and commitment to the task of developing a spirituality that would satisfy his hunger for an authentic experience of God is something that we can all share.

We shall see that Abhishiktānanda was not willing to pay 'lip service' to his faith in Jesus Christ, neither was he willing to simply ignore the richness and depth of the Hindu spiritual tradition that he encountered during his years in India. The intersection of these two powerful forces are what forged and tempered his faith, and of course these are the elements that make it so unique and worthy of study.

In the sections that follow we will consider both the formative 'external', contextual, realities that shaped and challenged his faith. Together with these we will also consider the 'internal', spiritual and psychological, factors that he wrestled with in his attempts to hold onto his faith in Christ, yet discover Christ with a new mystical depth that came from his life of contemplation and renunciation.

We begin with the outer journey

The *outer journey* – his life and context

Henri le Saux was born in St Briac, a small town on the north coast of Brittany, on the 30th of August 1910. He was the eldest of eight children in a devoutly Catholic family (Stuart 1989:1-2). From an early age Henri felt a calling to the priesthood. His parents encouraged his calling and sent him to the Minor Seminary at Châteaugiron in 1921. In 1926 he passed on to the Major Seminary in Rennes, France.

It was whilst he was at Rennes that the seed of his monastic vocation were sown.

Initially his parents were somewhat sceptical of their son becoming a monk – perhaps they would have preferred him to live the life of a parish priest rather than that of monk? However, he managed to win them over to the notion of his devout monastic call. Henri le Saux entered the Benedictine monastery at Kerognan soon after his 19th birthday in 1929 (Stuart 1989:6). He stayed there until he left the Abbey for India in 1948. It was there that he began his writings, the first being "Love and Wisdom," a study of the doctrine of the Trinity, a superb reflection that he had been working on since 1942. His writing always contained a large measure of self-disclosure, that is, according to Baumer-Despeigne "all that he writes is a direct reflection of his personal experience" (1983:311).

The importance of experience in the life and work of Henri (who later took on the name Abhishiktānanda) will become increasingly apparent in the section below.

Baumer-Despeigne notes a striking, and significant, fact that Abhishiktānanda's earliest writings, and the last entries into his diary before his death in 1973 (at the age of 63), both concern the Trinity (1983:311). However, as we shall discover, his understanding, and experience, of the mystery of the Trinity grew immensely throughout his life.

Henri's desire to go to India to establish a strictly contemplative monastery dates back to 1934, four years before his actual departure for India, however, this dream was not to come to fruition for some time (Stuart 1989:12). It was only after World War II, in 1945, that his Abbot gave him permission to approach various authorities about his desire. After he had received several initial positive responses from his Benedictine superiors, that later turned to negative, he was at the point of despair (Stuart 1989:13). Eventually, as Baumer-Despeigne notes, it was through a magazine article that he was put in touch with a French priest, Fr Jules Monchanin, "the pioneer of authentic dialogue with Hinduism" (1983:312). In response to this article Henri wrote a letter in French to the Bishop of Tiruchirappalli, the area in which Fr Monchanin was serving. Since the Bishop was unable to read French he had passed the letter on to Fr Monchanin for translation. And so the contact was made. Fr Monchanin had been living in India for some time already (since 1939) where he had been leading a life devoted to "the understanding and service of India, guided by a single desire: to incarnate Christianity in the ways of life, prayer and contemplation characteristic of Indian civilization." (Monchanin in Baumer-Despeigne 1983:312). Fr Monchanin responded to le Saux saying, "If you come, his Lordship is very willing for us to begin together a life of prayer, poverty and intellectual work" (in Stuart 1989:16). This positive response strengthened le Saux's resolve to go to India. In preparation for his departure he began to study English, Tamil and the Upanishads, and in addition he adopted a strictly vegetarian diet (Baumer-Despeigne 1983:312).

In a lengthy letter to Fr Monchanin, Dom le Saux put forward some basic principles for the realisation of their common project. These were: first, that he was not wanting to lay down any strict 'rule' (such as the Rule of St Benedict that is commonly followed in Benedictine Monasteries). Rather he indicated that for him "… a fundamental rule is adaption to circumstances and submission to reality" (in Stuart 1989:19). The next notion was that there must be total "Indianization." However, in spite of these two desires, their starting point would have to be the Rule of St Benedict (Stuart 1989:19). The reason for this was that it provided a monastic framework that was already tried and tested, and this would save them from having to "launch out into the unknown" (Stuart 1989:19). The Rule was however to be applied in a "very flexible and universal spirit" (Stuart 1989:19).

It was in this correspondence that le Saux revealed some further elements of his motivation for wanting to go to India. One of these desires was that he felt he had a task to "sanctify the whole contemplative thrust of India and Christianize the monastic institutions through which she expresses the depth of her spirit" (in Stuart 1989:19). This is a point that is well worth noting, since le Saux's theology develops, and changes, significantly in this regard throughout his life. We shall see how he begins to break free from the pressures and conventions of the Church, in later years, and moves on to far more radical understanding of what his spiritual task is.

Whereas he initially views Hinduism as needing to be 'Christianized', he later begins to see the need for Christianity to be 'Hinduized'. In other words, he understood that Christians could learn a great deal from the mystical devotion of the Hindus.

The final stage of his spiritual development, that would only take place much later in his life once he had lived in India for some time, would be the point of stressing that all religions need to be transcended in the quest of the Absolute.

Throughout his life one can discern three clear stages of spiritual development. His initial aim, as stated above, was to Christianize Hinduism. Then, he came to understand that Hinduism had some valuable insights to offer Christianity. Finally, he came to understand that neither religion could fully contain the truth of who and what God is. Thus, both conventional Christianity and conventional Hinduism would need to be transcended in order to experience the truth of the mystery of God.

Of course there needs to be a recognition that the earlier desires that we gleaned from his correspondence with Fr Monchanin show the naiveté of a person who has not yet encountered the culture that he is to embrace in India.

The intention of pointing out this shift is not to question it, but rather to highlight the fact that spiritual experiences often shift one's perceptions. Experience, as a necessary element of any 'lived' spirituality, broadens one's horizons as one comes to understand and integrate what was previously unknown. This was certainly the case with Henri le Saux.

In terms of his early aim, he envisaged the community taking shape in an ashram (or Indian / Christian monastery) where Hindus and Christians would come in search of nourishment for their spiritual selves. This encounter would be a first emphasis in their new venture. From the very earliest stages le Saux placed great emphasis on the ascetic nature of the monastic life. "Our life-style will certainly be very austere[3] much more so than is the case in our French Monasteries … we must live as *sannyasis*" (in Stuart 1989:21). A further emphasis in the community life, which is not surprising, was the traditional Benedictine virtue of manual labour (Stuart 1989:21). Their third emphasis was intellectual enrichment and study. This had the purpose of enabling "a rethinking of Christian dogma in Hindu terms, and Christian reinterpretation of Hindu thought" (in Stuart 1989:21). This

---

3   This means that they would live a very simple existence, a lifestyle that would be in keeping with the simplicity of the Hindus among whom they were living. What Benedictine monks in western monasteries might consider sacrificial living (i.e., eating three simple meals, sleeping in a bed, having a desk and chair for study in their cell etc.) would in fact be a luxurious lifestyle in India.

last task was the one that attracted him most, since it meant that the Christian gospel could be shared more effectively in Hindu terms, through the adaptation of Christian doctrine in familiar Indian symbols and philosophical concepts. Moreover, it was his intention to ensure that any Hindu elements of belief that were acceptable to Christianity could be incorporated into his own Christian faith.

He left the Abbey at Kerognan in 1948 and reached India on August 15 of that same year. In 1963 he was naturalised as an Indian citizen. He stayed in India until his death, at the age of 63, in 1973. In 1960 he became a naturalized Indian citizen (Baumer-Despeigne 1983:312).

Henri le Saux began his Indian initiation from the first day that he arrived at Kulittalai. Kulittalai is a town located in the Karur District and lies on the banks of the river Cauvery. It is about 30 km west of Tiruchirapalli and 25 km east of Karur.

Kulittalai is still a well-known center for pilgrimage with two important temples (Kadambavananathar Temple and Tiruveengoimalai Maragathachaleswarar Temple). This innitiation was to serve as preparation for the ashram life that he and Fr Monchanin hoped to lead. Stuart, who wrote a biography of Henri le Saux by studying his letters, writes that,

> He immersed himself enthusiastically in the life and culture
> of those whom he began to call 'my people', and above all
> sought direct contact with them in their spiritual experience.
> (Stuart 1989:25).

Stuart makes it clear that le Saux began to realise early on, that on an intellectual level Christianity and Hinduism were not compatible, and accordingly he made no attempts to strive for a merely superficial harmonisation of the two faiths (1989:32). This realisation of simple intellectual harmony marks the start of le Saux's spiritual struggle. From this point on he sought to immerse himself more deeply in the spirituality of Hinduism. One particular event that stands out in his early life was going to the *darshan*[4] of Sri Ramana Maharshi. In writing to his family about this event he writes that he made a

> ... Pilgrimage to a Hindu 'saint' who is regarded by Hindus
> as God himself. Extremely thought provoking. It is one of

---

4   The word, *darshan*, is a Hindi word meaning 'sight' or 'vision', associated with entering the presence of God or a saintly person.

the things that I would like to tell you about at length - when
I have the time. (in Stuart 1989:34).

The significance of this event will be discussed in greater detail below.

However, it is clear from this brief quote that he had already begun
to understand the significance of the Hindu faith for his spiritual
discovery and growth.

The founding of Shantivanam Ashram.

Along with Fr Monchanin, le Saux founded Shantivanam Ashram[5] in
1950 near Trichy in Tamil Nadu. This is a further significant aspect of
his spiritual journey, as we shall see, since it both laid the foundation
for those who would follow him (most notably Fr Bede Griffiths), and
also helped Henri to understand that his spiritual path was to be a
largely solitary one.

The Ashram was named 'Shantivanam', meaning Forest of peace,
because of its surroundings in a peaceful mango grove, on the banks of
the river Kavery (Stuart 1989:39). After six months of living in the
very meagre conditions at Shantivanam Henri le Saux wrote "We are
really living a hermit's life here. I would never have thought that my
dreams of 1934 would be so completely realized." (in Stuart 1989:41).

Furthermore in accordance with the custom of *sannyāsis* the two
monks took on Indian names. Jules Monchanin's name became
'*Paranama Arubiānanda*' meaning 'Bliss of the Supreme or Formless
One.' Dom le Saux took on the name '*Abhishikteshvarānanda*,' later
shortened to '*Abhishiktānanda*', meaning 'Bliss of the Anointed One,
the Lord' (Stuart 1989:40).

The ashram comprised two small huts and a chapel that was built
on the model of a Hindu temple (Baumer-Despeigne 1983:313). It was
a lonely retreat, and its aim had become much simpler than the initial
intention (discussed above). The aim of the ashram now was simply,
"… to be in the presence of God, without any further object at
all" (Stuart 1989:42). Note the shift from Abhishiktānanda's earlier
lofty ideals for the establishment of an ashram along Benedictine lines
to this simple and singular aim. Abhishiktānanda wrote about this,
saying that Shantivanam

---

5   An Ashram is a Hindu equivalent of the Christian monastery.

... could not consist in a more or less forced 'adaptation' of western Christian monasticism to the Indian context, but was nothing less than the assumption into the Church of the age-old Indian sannyasa itself. (in Stuart 1989:43).

The two 'monks' were attempting to live the life of true *sannyāsa*. They wore typical ochre coloured robes (known as 'kavi'), ate only vegetarian meals and spent a great deal of time in contemplation. It was in this atmosphere that the book "Hermits of *Saccidinanda*", an attempt at a Christian integration of the monastic tradition of India (1956) was written. By this time Abhishiktānanda had begun to immerse himself fully in the practice of Hindu spirituality through meditation, silence, and study of the sacred Hindu texts.

Besides the founding of Shantivanam Ashram, there are four further significant events in the life of Swāmi Abhishiktānanda. These are: first, was his relationship with Sri Gnānānanda, his guru, after 1956. Second, was his move to the Himalayas, which finally took place, in 1968. Third, was his *guru-shishya* (guru-disciple) relationship with the young Frenchman, Marc Chaduc. Finally, there is his heart attack and subsequent death in 1973. The effects and significance of these four events will be covered more extensively in the section that follows.

This cursory history traces the 'outer journey' of Swāmi Abhishiktānanda, in broad brush strokes, until his death. In order to understand the insights that Abhishiktānanda gained in India we must now move on to consider his 'inner' spiritual journey.

The *inner journey* - a move from within

Having considered how 'outer' circumstances formed and shaped Abhishiktānanda's developing spirituality, I thought it would be important to devote a complete subsection to the inner journey that was equally important in development of his unique approach to his faith. The reality is that a healthy spirituality always seeks to balance internal growth, reflection, and change, with the external circumstances . The interplay between inner and outer circumstances in Abhishiktānanda's life is thus very important to consider and understand if one is wishes to grasp what made his spiritual journey so unique and significant.

It is possible to understand Abhishiktānanda's approach to his spiritual (or inner) journey by examining one of his central convcitions.

Christianity will only become Indian - and thus universal -
by the integration into it of the contemplative dimension of
the Quest for the Absolute so characteristic of spiritual India.
(Baumer-Despeigne 1983:313).

Baumer-Despeigne qualifies this, correctly (as stated in the section
above), by saying that at first Abhishiktānanda was convinced that in
Christianity, as he had come to understand and appreciate it within its
'western', Catholic, Monastic, guise, there was an expression of the
fullness of all truth. Accordingly he believed that it was thus only a
matter of presenting this 'truth' in a manner that would make it
acceptable to the Indian cultural mindset (Baumer-Despeigne
1983:313). However, as he began to penetrate the Indian religious
experience, this simplistic understanding of real truth began to change.
It is thus not surprising for him to write that "Truth has to be taken
from wherever it comes; that is Truth possess us - we do not possess
Truth" (Abhishiktānanda in Baumer-Despeigne 1983:313).

Characteristic of Abhishiktānanda's spirituality, as is common in
mystical, and Hindu spiritualities, is his emphasis on the primacy of
experience (anubhāva). Essentially

he maintained that spiritual practice, and experience of the divine,
take precedence over theological formulation (stated more simply,
what we know about God is less important than knowing God). This is
a perfectly sensible position to take since all theology is ultimately a
discovery of what God reveals to humanity, not what the human person
discovers about God as a result of his or her own volition. However,
this experiential approach caused him great struggle and turmoil as he
tried to reconcile his loyalty to the 'cerebral' doctrines of his Christian
faith within the context of new and powerful experiences in his
developing spiritual journey. This process, and the struggle that
accompanied it, will be discussed below.

What is worth noting is that an unconventional spiritual path will
often lead the seeker through some measure of insecurity and turmoil.
It is easy to follow convention and build upon the foundations of what
others have discovered. However, uncharted spiritual territories remain
to be discovered. The depth and breadth and magnitude of God's
loving revelation can never be fully realised by just one single
approach to faith. What is certain is that when one has the courage to

look for God in new and uncommon ways, the rewards of discovery can be great!

Abhishiktānanda's inner journey can be divided roughly into six phases. These are not necessarily chronological movements (as with the 'outer journey' discussed above). At times he struggled with many things at once. However, in my view there are six 'shaping events' influencing his spirituality and theology along his faith journey to the 'Further Shore', and his eventual rediscovery of the wonderful mystery of the Triune God just before his death in 1973.

Sri Ramana Maharshi and the caves at Tiruvannāmalai

The first significant spiritual change took place very shortly after Dom le Saux's arrival in India (1949). This is the shift from seeing Christianity, as a religion and theological structure of faith, that possesses and contains all truth, to realising that "Truth has to be taken from wherever it comes ..." (Abhishiktānanda in Baumer-Despeigne 1983:313). It is this shift, from the particularity of Christian truth to an understanding that God's mysterious truth is greater than just one faith, that causes him to remark "I am not a missionary, but a poor Christian monk in the midst of Hindu monks" (in Stuart 1989:63).

Probably the most significant influence upon him during this period were a number of encounters with a sage (jnāni[6]) of the sacred mountain, Arunāchala. Henri le Saux writes of these encounters with Sri Ramana Maharshi,

> Even before my mind was able to recognize the fact, and still
> less to express it, the invisible halo of this Sage had been
> perceived by something in me deeper than any words... In
> the sage of Arunāchala ... I discerned the Unique Sage of the
> eternal India ... it was as if the very soul of India penetrated
> to the very depths of my own soul and held mysterious
> communion with it. It was a call which pierced through

---

6   A jnāni is a person who has come to a true 'self realisation', i.e., the mystical and spiritual realisation that God and God's creation are not 'ontologically' separate. Rather, God dwells within all of God's creation, since that is how the creation comes into being, gains its life, and is sustained in life. The realisation that the 'self' and the 'other' are not separate is central Abhishiktānanda's spirituality, as we shall see in later sections.

everything, rent it in pieces and opened a mighty abyss... (le
Saux in Baumer-Despeigne 1983:313).

As a result of the influence of these significant encounters with Sri
Ramana Maharshi, Henri began to ask questions, to wrestle and
struggle within himself, and wrestle with these powerful new
experiences. If the Christian faith as he knew it was the fullness of
truth, then what was he to make of his new experiences of God, and
Truth, that he encountered with Sri Ramana? He writes, "... these
powerful new experiences ... with the Maharshi ... new as they were,
their hold on me was already too strong for it ever to be possible for
me to disown them" (le Saux in Stuart 1989:34).

He goes on to write in his diary that, "the ashram of Ramana helps
me to understand the Gospel; there is in the Gospel much more than
Christian Piety has so far discovered" (in Baumer-Despeigne
1983:313). Here the shift toward a discovery of truth in the Hindu
religion is evident. This encounter with truth through the *jnāni* moves
him to realise that Christianity can learn from God's revelation through
the spirituality of India.

Sri Ramana died in 1950. Nevertheless, even after the sage's death,
Abhishiktānanda often came back between 1952 and 1958 to spend
extended periods in different caves on the holy mountain, living as a
Christian hermit among Hindu hermits. Bruteau suggests that he was
drawn by the mountain itself, where traditionally Lord Shiva is said to
have manifest himself as a column of fire and light (1994:302). This
was clearly a very important and significant time in Abhishiktānanda's
life. Baumer-Despeigne notes that it was in the silence and solitude of
the caves that his first "great spiritual breakthrough came" (1983:314).
In his diary Abhishiktānanda writes about the emergence of this
spiritual realisation.

> The entry into one's own nature is equivalent to the reaching
> of the Deity in the depth of oneself, a descent to the level at
> which one is nothing but the Image of God ... Ramana's
> advaita is my birth place. Against that all rationalization is
> shattered... So what is to be done? Only one thing. If the
> Christian mystery is true, it will reappear intact on the other
> side of the non-dualistic experience. (in Baumer-Despeigne
> 1983:314).

The primacy of 'spiritual experience', that was brought about through meditation, learning from his encounters with Hindu sages, together with supernatural encounters with the mysterious truth of God (in visions, and dreams), are perhaps one of the most characteristic aspects of Abhishiktānanda's spirituality from this point onwards. His concern was not to remain with the pointers to God (religions), but to pass beyond these symbols to a non-dual[7] (*advaitin*) experience of God. A foundational characteristic of his spirituality, and theology, at this point was this: If Christianity embodied truth, the same truth that he was encountering in his spiritual discovery in India, it would be found intact when he reached the 'other side'. Essentially the experience of not being separate from God became so foundational to his spirituality that it surpassed the importance of allegiance to the doctrinal truths of the Christian faith. If the doctrines of Christianity were true, in any sense, they would be proven so by his experience of them in experiencing God.

This leads to the second significant shift in his spirituality and theology.

Spiritual rebirth: The move beyond the commonly held boundaries of Christianity

The spiritual awakening, or re-birth that was discussed in the previous section, led Abhishiktānanda beyond the conventional boundaries of Christian spirituality and faith for a portion of his spiritual journey. This statement does warrant some clarification. First, it must be emphasised that orthodoxy is a difficult concept to define. What some consider orthodox in one setting may be consider as radically unorthodox in another. For example, many in the West may find Abhishiktānanda's unconventional appearance and lifestyle somewhat difficult to relate to their understanding of Christianity. However, we need to be sure that by the same standards there are many Africans, Indians, and Latin American, and Indian Christians who find the opulence of designer suits and Church's that resemble shopping malls to be incongruent with the values of the Gospel.

---

7   Non-duality is not so much a singular experience of being one with God, since this assumes that there are 2 beings to begin with (a 'self' and God's 'self') who are united. Rather non-duality in this sense refers to a lack of being separated from God in whom all things '…live and move and have their being' (Acts 17:28).

So, context is important. Second, it must be remembered that even though Abhishiktānanda's spirituality came to bear little resemblance to conventional Christian symbols (for parts of his spiritual journey) he never wavered on the central awareness of the mystery of the Triune God. Regardless of these qualifications it must be granted that his Christian faith was being stretched and refined by Sri Ramana's vedantic philosophy, the experience of *advaita* i.e., non-duality. For some this crossing to the 'further shore' of Hindu philosophy does present an instance of breaking with mainline orthodox Christian spirituality. Abhishiktānanda describes this transformation as follows.

> In my own innermost centre ... I tried to discover the image of him whose I am, of him who lives and reigns in the infinite space (*akasha*) of my heart. But the reflected image gradually grew faint, and soon it was swallowed up in the radiance of the Original ... I descended into what seemed to me to be successive depths of my true self ... Finally nothing was left but he himself, the Only One, infinitely alone, Being, Awareness and Bliss, *Saccidananda*. In the heart of *Saccidananda* I had returned to my Source (1990:172).

Swāmi Abhishiktānanda had realised the supreme ideal of Hinduism, that is, the absolute surrender of self (the ego), to the inner Mystery of God. He had learned where and how to seek God who is the only true and Ultimate Reality, and this discovery was not to be found outside of himself, as many western spiritualities assume. The search was not for some unreachable transcendent God, as is often undertaken by Christians, particularly those from the Reformed Christian traditions of the West, where the emphasis of spirituality rests far more acutely upon a realisation of the 'otherness' and transcendence of God. Rather, he had found the Ultimate Mystery to be contained in the very centre of his being, that is, in that place that he often referred to as the *cave of the heart* (*guhā*) (Abhishiktānanda 1984:10). A poem that he wrote during this period illustrates his discovery of the need for introspection.

> I abide in this secret place in the depth of my heart, there -
> where all alone before God I am,
> where all alone with God I am,
> where all alone from God I am,
> where alone is He who IS.
> *(From Ermite du Saccidananda 1956:81, in Baumer-Despeigne 1983:316).*

So, this second significant spiritual discovery was a realisation that the mystery of God can be discovered and encountered within the human 'self', since the mysterious, powerful, and all loving God was not only transcendent, but also immanent. In other words, whilst one can find God in nature, in meditation upon the scriptures, through liturgy, worship, and prayer, one could also discover the mystery of God in the 'cave' of one's own heart.

Guru and disciple: a seal on Abhishiktānanda's initiation into the spirituality of the Upanishads

The third definitive stage in Abhishiktānanda's spiritual journey was his introduction to Sri Gnānānanda in 1956. Sri Gnānānanda was a Hindu sage (*jnāni* – one who has come to true 'self realisation') with a non-dualistic, mystical, approach to spirituality that was quite similar to that of Sri Ramana (Baumer-Despeigne 1983:316). The central teaching of this jnāni is that, the "only thing that matters is that one casts off all that hinders one from giving oneself utterly and completely to this silent meditation in the depth of one's being" (Abhishiktānanda 1974:89), that is, a life of absolute renunciation or *sannyāsa*[8].

"The meeting with a guru," according to Abhishiktānanda,

> ...is the essential meeting, the decisive turning point in the life of a man ... in the meeting of the guru and disciple there is no longer even fusion, for we are on the plane of the original non-duality ... What the guru says springs from the very heart of the disciple. It is not that another is speaking to him... (1974:29-30).

Abhishiktānanda had recognised in this *jnāni* one who has "penetrated to his very source and has known the secret of himself and the mystery of God in his manifestation" (in Vattakuzhy 1981:110). The guru passes on to his disciples the realisation that he (the guru) has attained. "The disciple is united to God through his guru... The guru is for him

---

8   This word can be both a verb and a noun. As a verb it refers to the action of renouncing, i.e., letting go off, or negating, all things that hinder spiritual progress or growth (such as possessions, desires, etc.). As a noun it refers to persons who have taken up this path of renunciation. The Hindu *sannyāsi* is usually a male who devotes himself entirely to the discovery of the mystical reality of God (in some sense he could be likened to a wondering, ascetic, monk).

an authentic revelation of God" (Journal 3.4.52 in Edwards 1997:13). This realisation had a significant effect on Abhishiktānanda's Christology, particularly as his Christology relates to his spirituality. This notion will be discussed in much greater detail in a later section of the book.

In order to work through all that he had learnt from, and experienced with, Sri Ramana, Sri Gnānānanda, and his time on Arunāchala, Abhishiktānanda undertook a 32 day retreat at Kumbakonam[9] (Baumer-Despeigne 1983:316). This was a time of further inner anguish. He was continually torn between his loyalty to the notion of the Christ as 'supremely other', and transcendently divine, that he had become accustomed to as a western Christian, and the overwhelming vedantic experience, of non-dualism between the 'self' and the 'God of the self'. Together with this experience was the anxiety that he may be relying too much on his guru, a human person, in the quest for the divine. This anguish moved him to cry:

> I am afraid, I am afraid, an ocean of anguish wherever I turn.
> I am afraid of risking eternity for a mirage. And yet, no! You
> are not a mirage, Arunachala; and the light of dawn which
> has risen at the centre of my heart is not false … Agonies
> which pierce me to the depths and make my soul just a cry of
> pain!!! (in Baumer-Despeigne 1983:317).

However, the breakthrough can be marked where he writes in his diary three days later, on 30 November 1956, "Christ is my *Sadguru* - my true Guru…" (in Baumer-Despeigne 1983:317). It would naïve to say that this shift did away with the tension that existed within himself between these two loyalties, the loyalty to the traditional western-Christian notion of Christ, and this new discovery of Christ as his *sadguru*. When one reads his diary and journal one can see glimpses of this tension resurfacing at various points until his eventual heart attack in 1973, the event that was finally to "carry him off forever to the Further Shore" (Baumer-Despeigne 1983:317).

---

9   **Kumbakonam** is a city and a municipality in the Thanjavur district in the Indian state of Tamil Nadu. Kumbakonam is called as temple town because of the large number of temples within the town and the nearby areas. It is thus considered a sacred and holy place, where many seekers would go on pilgrimage as they sought to find guidance, truth, and inner realization.

Edwards records a clear example of this struggle in Abhishiktānanda in her paper. The event is a conversation between H W L Poonja and Abhishiktānanda. Poonji and Abhishiktānanda met on Arunāchula. Poonji taught the same direct spiritual path as Sri Ramana Maharshi, "the practice of constant inquiry into the self (ātmavichāra)" (Edwards 1997:15). The conversation reads as follows:

Abhishiktānanda	"How far am I from enlightenment?"
Poonja	"As far as the sky from the earth."
Abhishiktānanda	"What is stopping me?"
Poonja	"That bag on the shoulder. Throw it into the Ganga."
Abhishiktānanda	"I can't."

According to Edwards Poonjaji felt that the bag represented "Christian trappings which Abhishiktānanda was unnecessarily holding on to" (1997:16). It takes great courage to go reshape one's life and one's faith. I am fairly certain that we can all identify with the the struggle that is described above. For Abhishiktānanda his path towards enlightenment meant casting of the security of the few possessions that he was carrying with him in his bag (among which were the traditional tools of Christian spirituality, such as a Bible, and a book of prayers and liturgies). For some of us the path towards truth may mean casting off some of the subtle comforts that we treasure, such a familiar manner of worship, or a particular approach to prayer, it might even mean that we have to make some concrete choices about our lifestyle, what work we do, what relationships we are in, and who we perceive ourselves to be. It was only in casting off all that kept Abhishiktānanda within the 'familiar' framework of his life and faith that he could find the freedom to make new discoveries, and venture into deeper and more meaningful aspects of God's mysterious truth.

This challenge will face all serious seekers at some stage in their spiritual journey. Perhaps you might consider what keeps you from making bold new spiritual discoveries?

The death of Jules Monchanin: Moving away from Shantivanam to the Himalayas

The death of Fr Monchanin was another decisive "turning point" in the life and spirituality of Abhishiktānanda (Baumer-Despeigne 1983:317). As mentioned above, their initial hope had been to start an ashram, a monastery with a Hindu Christian character. Sadly, however, very few Indian Christians had come to join the ashram. Some had tried it, but none had ever stayed on.

My observation is that this is often the case with fresh cultural expressions of faith. Whilst outsiders often find richness and depth in a local culture, the indigenous population have often become disillusioned, or perhaps just too accustomed, to the elements of that culture to find it engaging and enchanting. Rather, they long for something different. This lack of response by the local population caused Abhishiktānanda to concentrate more and more on a life of *sannyāsa* (total renunciation), free from all possessions, free to wander.

In a letter to his sister, he wrote about his journeys saying:

> I have been making a marvellous journey ... among the Himalayas ... It is marvellous to travel on foot ... One is free... There is an enchanting solitude ... I stayed for several days at Hardwar, just at this meeting point [where the Ganges runs into the plains]. It is a ceaseless pilgrimage... The Himalayas have conquered me. (in Baumer-Despeigne 1983:318).

From this time on he was to divide his time between Shantivanam ashram in the South, and the mountains in the North. Abhishiktānanda finally settled in the North at Uttarkashi on the banks of the sacred river Ganges in 1968. He had begun to build a small shelter for himself here in 1959. It was close to the final stopping place before the principal source of the Ganges. In another letter to his sister he wrote,

> What a beautiful place ... at Uttarkashi sadhus (monks) are everywhere ... Solitude. The noise of the river drowns all other sounds. The world is wholly forgotten, nothing distracts one from what is essential... (Baumer-Despeigne 1983:319).

It was here that he began to seek a more precise definition of the spiritual experience of *advaita*. The following extract from a letter to his friend Odette Baumer-Despeigne, who is often quoted in this book. The letter is dated January 1968 and illustrates Abhishiktānanda's quest.

> I more and more believe that the deepening of the spiritual sense is the only remedy for the present crisis in the Churches. What we really need is a theology which meditates on the mysteries of the faith, no longer as mere concepts - after the fashion inherited from the Greeks - but by starting directly from the experience of the Self which is at the centre of every Indian spiritual tradition. (in Baumer-Despeigne 1983:320).

This was a time for casting off the unnecessary elements of his Christian faith (i.e., those elements of the faith that were non-essential, such as the elements that come from particular cultural expressions of Christianity). Abhishiktānanda was carefully passing beyond the mere symbols of religion toward realisation of the Ultimate truth of the faith within himself. This was largely a time of freedom, freedom from the constraints upon his time and energy that were imposed upon him by the structured life of the ashram. Now Abhishiktānanda was truly living as a Hindu *sannyāsi* yet as a Christian, seeking to renounce everything that hindered his discovery of Triune God. This was a time of great introspection, consolidating and a deepening of his spirituality. The events of his outer life, the time spent in India, his growth as a *sannyāsi*, the time in the ashram and in the mountains, had begun to have a marked effect upon his 'inner life.' To look at him, and to consider the structure of his life, one could quite easily mistake him for a Hindu. However, he remained committed to Christ, rather than Christianity, and his life was marked by deep and sincere devotion to meditating upon the new discoveries of the mystery of God that he was making during this period.

In 1964 Abhishiktānanda, along with Raimundo Pannikar, had undergone a pilgrimage to Gangotri which is close to the source of the Ganges river, a river that is considered to be holy in Hindu religion. Just as he had gone to Gangotri to be closer to the source of the Holy Ganges, so too he indicated that he had moved there to come closer to his True Source. He writes of this saying,

> I climbed to the source of the Ganges. Whatever man may be below in the plains, here he is nothing more than a pilgrim

returning to God, to himself, to the silence from which he
has sprung (in Edwards 1997:20).

This shift to the inner life, that was initiated through his move to the
Himalayas, was now a primary focus of his spiritual pursuit. It would
remain so until his death in 1973.

The shift: From disciple to guru

The above-mentioned move created a climate within which
Abhishiktānanda began to struggle with another aspect of his life. On
the one hand he felt the strong call to solitude and contemplation. On
the other hand he had a strong desire to share his experiences with
others. He writes,

> I find myself truly cornered between the call to non-action
> from my *sadhu* neighbours and the call to speak, write,
> testify, which comes to me from so many Christian friends.
> This life of compromise is not at all restful. But the
> compromise itself should develop into unity. (Letter to
> Odette Baumer-Despeigne 1969, in Baumer-Despeigne
> 1983:322-323).

This is another vivid example of how Abhishiktānanda's inner life is
affected by his outer life. His desire to share meant that he had to travel
from his place of solitude and have human contact, such contact broke
into his solitude affecting the depth of his spiritual life. Initially the
human contacts created a sense of disease, however, as seen above he
believed that the compromise of meeting with other people and
breaking his introspection would eventually develop into a greater
unity (Baumer-Despeigne 1983:323). It is important to recognise that
the overarching doctrinal theme of his spiritually was that of the Holy
Trinity, a relationship of mystery, in which some measure of common
life, yet life in absolute devotion, was necessary. This inner struggle
begins to shape his understanding of the need for a life lived with
others, yet absolutely and totally devoted to God. In some sense one
can see the completion of the cycle of community based spirituality
forming in this aspect of his spiritual journey. He starts his faith
journey as a Benedictine monk whose identity and life is shaped by the
common life of the community, moves almost entirely into solitude,
and then is slowly drawn back into a deeper and more significant,
although intensely difficult, understanding of the need for community.

The epitome of his transformation in this regard takes place in the remarkable relationship that developed after 1971 between Abhishiktānanda, two young Hindu men, and "Marc Chaduc, a young Frenchman" (Baumer-Despeigne 1983:324).

Abhishiktānanda said of this relationship, "In him [Chaduc] I have found a true and wholehearted disciple; with two young Hindus I have experienced from the other end what a guru is" (in Baumer-Despeigne 1993:324). Between these men a true *guru-shishya* (guru-disciple) relationship developed as Abhishiktānanda began to function more and more as a guru, passing on his discovery and growing enlightenment to his disciples. Edwards writes "With this young Frenchman he shared the depths of what he had learned and what he had attained" (1997:22).

Edwards notes that it was only in immersing himself with Marc in an existential study of the Upanishads in preparation for Marc's initiation into *sannyāsa* (total renunciation) that Abhishiktānanda was able to experience fully the *advaita* or non-duality that the Upanishads convey (1997:22). In sharing his experience of realization with his disciple, a *kenōsis* or self-emptying takes place, a further step in the journey of renunciation – a renunciation of holding on to what is 'self'. He shares all that he is with his disciple, it is an emptying of the Self, moving beyond the ego.

In May 1972 Abhishiktānanda and his disciple stayed together for almost a month on the banks of the Ganges. During this time they devoted themselves to "the meditative study of the Upanishads" (Baumer-Despeigne 1983:326). They moved ever deeper, inward. Abhishiktānanda described the experience as follows:

> Days of extraordinary fullness - an intoxicating experience of the truth of the Upanishads, even if for me one that was physically shattering; the whole ground of the spirit heaves up, as when deep strata heave up from the bottom and make to ocean boil. To feel oneself in the Presence of the True is too powerful and experience. It scorches one! (Letter to Odette Baumer-Despeigne 1972, in Baumer-Despeigne 1983:326).

The above mentioned study had led him to write:

> This study of the demands of *Sannyasa* has certainly struck me forcibly... It reminds me of how astounded King Josiah was when the priests discovered in a corner of the Temple an

old manuscript of Deuteronomy which appeared to have been completely forgotten ... when he realized the requirements of belonging to the 'chosen people' he was simply knocked down. (letter to SwāmiAjatānanda (or Marc Chaduc) in Baumer-Despeigne 1983:327).

Marc Chaduc's (Swāmi Ajatānanda) initiation into *sannyāsa* took place on 30 June 1973 in the holy river Ganges at Rishikesh. It was presided over by both a Christian (Abhishiktānanda) and a Hindu (Swāmi Chidānanda of Rishikesh). Abhishiktānanda was deeply moved by this ceremony and by the study of the Upanishads that had preceded it. He expresses some of this emotion in the following poem written for Marc.

In reclothing you with the kavi,
and beholding you reclothed,
I discovered
that the kavi was not merely a sign,
but a mystery,
the explosion outwardly
of the tejomaya Purusha [the Man of glory],
of the depths of Being.
(Poem to Marc Chaduc 5.7.73 in Stuart 1989:341).

Thus, the guru-disciple relationship charts another significant development in Abhishiktānanda's developing spirituality. Through this experience he comes to realise both the need for unity with other persons (i.e., a spirituality that is formed in community, much like the community that is present in the life of the Trinity), but also the need to share his growth and development with others (again, this is a mirror of the *perichoretic*, self emptying, nature of the persons of the Trinity who gives themselves over to one another completely).

The final stage: Moving to the Further Shore

Two weeks after the initiation of Chaduc, having shared in some time of "marvellously ecstatic consolidation with Marc", Abhishiktānanda had a heart-attack whilst running to catch a bus at a bazaar in Rishikesh (Edwards 1997:24). For Abhishiktānanda his heart-attack was a time of much greater "awakening" (Stuart 1989:345). Once again the interplay between what happened in Abhishiktānanda's outer and inner life is notable. Abhishiktānanda interpreted the heart attack in the context of his recent spiritual experience. He articulated this in a letter to Marc, one week after the attack.

> I have to recognize that a 'Force' passes through being [beings?] … which is terribly dangerous. For my affair was not so much the result of stupidly running after a bus, as the upshot of those two weeks, the explosion of which the poem spoke. (Letter to Marc Chaduc 21.7.73 in Stuart 1989:345, [beings?] added by Stuart).

He felt that the heart attack had allowed him at last to move beyond the struggle that he had been engaged in for so many years. He was free from concern about the body, free from inward and outer inconsistencies, it was truly a spiritual breakthrough. He later recorded the experience of the heart attack in the following manner.

> It was a marvellous spiritual experience. The discovery that the awakening has nothing to do with any situation, even so-called life or so-called death; one is awake and that is all. While I was waiting on the sidewalk, on the frontier of the two worlds, I was magnificently called, for I AM, no matter in what world! I have found the grail! (Letter to his family 15.8.73 in Stuart 1989:346).

The realisation was that each and every person in their situation can have this awakening wherever they are (Edwards 1997:24). "This means that awakening is not so much a matter of attaining … as of realizing that the Source, the goal to be attained, … can be accessed from anywhere, any time" (Edwards 1997:24).

At last it seemed that the intense struggle in *Swāmiji* was over. There was no longer any struggle between the outer and inner worlds, between *advaita* and Christ. He had found fulfilment as a Christian *sannyāsi*. There was no longer any conflict between his loyalty to Christ and the vedantic experience. Abhishiktānanda expressed this in saying, "the Trinity is an experience, not a *theologoumenon*… The Trinity is the ultimate mystery of the Self" and, "All notions are burnt in the fire of experience" (Abhishiktānanda in Edwards 1997:24). He had realised that all concepts were to be transcended, *advaita* and *dvaita*, duality and non-duality, Christianity and Hinduism, these were all merely conceptual, and needed to be transcended toward incorporation in the One True Mystery. Abhishiktānanda died on

7 December 1973. Baumer-Despeigne writes of this final stage in
Abhishiktānanda's journey:

> The pilgrim to the "Further Shore" had reached his goal, his
> whole being was now harmonized, unified at peace; entirely
> faithful to Christ his *Sadguru* and wholly immersed in the
> depths of his soul, in his "ground", he had "returned to his
> Source." His Christian experience and the Upanhishadic
> experience had flowed back to their unique Origin. (Baumer-
> Despeigne 1983:329).

Conclusion

When I first encountered the writings of Abhishiktānanda I was struck
by two somewhat contradictory reactions within myself.

My first reaction was one that is probably quite common among
contemporary Christians from a western, reformed or evangelical,
perspective – I was unsure, and even unsettled, by his bold steps to
search for God beyond conventional Christian spirituality. As I think
about this reaction some years later I am not surprised that I reacted in
that manner. Unfortunately a great deal of contemporary Christianity
encourages believers to 'fit in', not to challenge the status quo, and
certainly not to seek to discover new things about God and the
Christian faith outside of Christianity! In my mind the only possible
way of deepening one's spirituality was through the attendance of
Church worship services, daily devotional reading and prayer, and
occasionally subjecting myself to a short guided retreat, or some form
of centring prayer.

My second, and almost simultaneous, reaction to Abhishiktānanda's
spirituality was a sense of excitement and admiration. I was excited
because I had encountered a level of integrity and courage in
Abhishiktānanda's spiritual quest that was so lacking in my
conventional faith. He was pushing the boundaries, charting new paths,
doing things that were daring and challenging, and what was most
impressive for me, was that he had the courage to embark upon this
uncertain journey in the hope that he would develop a real and
significant encounter with the God whom he loved and served. I
admired his courage. It caused me to reconsider my own lack of
courage. I could identify with his fears and struggles. I too wanted to

find a way to relate to God within a new, and rich, context. However, my context was not India, but Africa. I too was dissatisfied with the shallow and commonplace expressions and experiences of faith that I encountered around me. Yet, there was something so comfortable about clinging to what was know, and something so frightening about passing beyond these familiar and comfortable forms and symbols in the pursuit of greater and more meaningful spiritual truth.

As I suggest in the introduction to this book, you may find some of the 'external' manifestations of Abhishiktānanda's spiritual quest to be strange and unfamiliar, however, what I hope you have seen in this chapter is his sincerity and integrity. He sincerely loved Jesus Christ, in fact he loved Christ so much that he was not willing to settle for an 'image' of Christ. Rather, he would do what others would consider strange, and even unacceptable, in order to come to a fuller and more real experience of the Lord. So, he adapted his 'outward' life to that of the Hindu monks. Yet, he was also brave enough to challenge himself to make 'inward," spiritual, changes in order to get closer to his goal of knowing the Triune God more intimately and fully.

I wish there were more courageous pioneers like this; more ardent seekers who will have the courage to brave the unknown, and the unfamiliar, in the pursuit of worthwhile spiritual discoveries. We should never forget that what we regard as 'normal' and 'ordinary' today was unconventional, and often even persecuted, rejected, and misunderstood in its own time. This list could include such examples as Martin Luther and John Calvin during the Reformation, persons such as John Wesley and the early pioneers of the Holiness movements in 18th century England, and even some contemporary examples such as the 'Black theologies' of James Cone, and the Latin American Liberation Theologians, Gustavo Guitierrez and Leonardo Boff – the list could go on and on.

If we are honest, those of us who belong to 'regular' Churches recognise that the Church, and even our religious approach to the Lord of the Church, needs to change. I have seldom met a Christian who is entirely at peace with their Church, denomination, or spiritual approach. Being willing to change the way we worship, pray, share the Gospel, and find meaning and hope together, could be one of the most courageous and necessary things that we do for ourselves and future generations. In order to do this we will need to develop the courage to look for Christ in the unfamiliar places, among different people, in ancient and less dominant cultures, and through various expressions of faith. It is just such courage that characterises Abhishiktānanda's unique spirituality.

A critical consideration of the characteristics of Henri le Saux's unconventional spirituality

In the previous section we familiarised ourselves with some of the more important stages in the development of Abhishiktānanda's spirituality. Having done so we will go on to outline, discuss, and consider the actual content and characteristics of his unconventional approach to discovering, and living within, the mystery of God.

As has already been discussed, a great deal of Abhishiktānanda's spirituality developed out of his intense personal struggle to reconcile his loyalty to Christ and Christianity, on the one hand, with the experiences of *advaita* and his life as a *sannyāsi* in India, on the other.

In order to effectively discuss and consider the characteristic elements of this complex and uncommon spirituality it will be necessary to outline and explain, not only the various components of his spirituality, but also to examine the theological concepts that underpin them whilst offering some critical insight into the content and development of these elements. In some cases it will be necessary to give a brief explanation of the history and development of certain concepts for a clearer understanding of them. This may be particularly necessary with regards to practices and beliefs that stem from Hinduism, since it is assumed that the primary readership of this book will be enquiring Christians who may not necessarily be informed about some of the more subtle elements of Hindu faith and spiritual life. It his hoped that as we come to understand the origins, and constituent foci of Swāmi Abhishiktānanda's spirituality, that we will gain an understanding of the valuable contribution that his groundbreaking work offers Hindu Christian encounter and the deepening of fresh expressions of Christian spirituality.

Although we shall consider each of these characteristic elements separately it must be kept in mind they were not separated and distinct in the life of Abhishiktānanda, rather each of these elements formed part of a single integrated whole. However, for the sake of our task it is necessary to introduce some structural separation for the sake of clarity and examination.

A spirituality of experience

The most distinctive feature of the spirituality of Abhishiktānanda is that it is based not merely on the study of theological concepts and doctrines – as is often the case in many Western Christian traditions. Rather, his spirituality is based predominantly on mystical and spiritual experience. It is in the face of this mystical experience that, for him, all else was relativised - all names and forms or *namarupa* (that is all myths and symbols, images and concepts), were merely relative symbolic representations of a far greater truth that could be experienced, yet not completely or adequately explained. It was this element of discovery that caused him so much distress. He constantly battled to reconcile his transcendent experience of God with the inadequate symbols and expressions of doctrine that he had been taught to believe were complete expressions of the truth of God. It is worth noting that this dichotomy between experience and reason (or more particularly the dichotomy between spiritual discovery and doctrinal formulation), is quite common among Christians in cultures that are more experiential in nature. For example, my first year systematic theology students here in South Africa seem to struggle much more acutely with the Greek philosophy that underpins the doctrinal formulations of Christ's divinity and humanity. However, their experience of Jesus as a human person, who is fully God, is much more vivid and tangible.

The effects of Hellenism and Greek philosophy in the formulation of Christian doctrine, which in itself was often a reaction to heretical ideas, has left later Christians with a complex maze of ideas, words, symbols, and concepts that mean very little in contemporary society. This is particularly true for Christians in cultures and contexts that have very little historical connection with the philosophy of ancient Greece. Throughout its history western Christianity has emphasised an ascent to 'ideas', 'symbols', and 'doctrines', as a primary expression of orthodoxy (knowing and believing the truth). A common example of this problem is to be found in the attaching of notions of gender to the persons of the godhead, i.e., if one were to ask a sampling of Christians in America, or England, whether God is male or female, most would assume that God is 'male' since the language and symbolism of scripture and the later doctrines that form the corpus of Christian tradition use this symbolic language to refer to the first person of the trinity. Sadly, those who *experience* God as 'mother' are often branded as heretics at worst, or liberals at best.

In the case of Swāmi Abhishiktānanda's spirituality he asked how he could hold onto a form of Christianity that has such a fundamental emphasis on these symbolic 'names' and 'forms.' The struggle was accentuated by the fact that our symbolic language always uses the symbols of this world (e.g., maleness or femaleness) to try and explain truths and realities that ultimately transcend all symbolic explanation.

In order to examine how this aspect of experience came to dominate Abhishiktānanda's spirituality it is important to understand and consider the context in which his spirituality began to transform from reason to experience.

The experience of 'Ultimate Reality' in the East

One of the greatest differences between the eastern and the western mindset is what informs each one's notion of what is truly 'Real'. Westerners generally tend to be aware only of the conscious, rational, and material worlds. Truth in these worlds are most often discovered through science, understood through reason, and expressed with logic. Conversely the Indian, or more specifically the Hindu person, tends to live more easily from the unconscious and intuitive dimension of the soul (Griffiths 1982:8). The outer, manifest world, is seen as *maya* (illusion) or as a product of *avidya* (ignorance). What is 'Real' is not discovered by scientific and empirical investigation, but rather by spiritual experience, that is, the truth of reality is discovered through spiritual introspection.

One can trace the concepts underlying this second view of reality as spiritual truth in the following manner: It begins with the assertion that *brahman*, the Reality that is behind all phenomena, is One with the Reality behind human consciousness (that is *ātman*). Dom Bede Griffiths, who was a successor to Swāmi Abhishiktānanda, elaborates on this concept as follows,

> Whether we move from the outer world to discover the Reality behind it, or from the inner world to discover the reality within, we encounter this one Reality, the *brahman*, or the *ātman*, the Self, as it is called. (Griffiths 1989:177).

Thus, the outcome is that an experience of the Ultimate Reality is far more important than a mere understanding of it. Moreover, an experience that is based on anything other than the Ultimate Reality is based on an illusion (*maya*). Thus, for the Hindu, experience of the Ultimate reality is far more profitable than a reasoned exposition of doctrines and beliefs. Experience is more highly regarded than scientific investigation and the gathering of facts to prove this or that point. It is from this understanding that Abhishiktānanda writes, "in every moment there should be a conscious search for the real self through all that is done, thought or said." (1989:42).

There is something quite sensible and significant in this emphasis. I am fairly certain that most Christians would agree that the symbols that we use to express the mystery of who and what God truly is will always be inadequate to capture the entire truth of God's person and nature. This does not mean that doctrine is unnecessary or a useless pursuit. Of course one does need to strive to understand and express one's experience with accuracy, vivid symbolism, and meticulous care – that is, after all, how elements of the faith are passed from one generation to the next. However, what one must guard against is an overemphasis on reason and knowledge as the foundations of truth. One of my students recently commented, after a rather heated debate in our theology class, that Christianity in the West seems to have a new motto: *and now all that remains is faith, hope, and love – and the greatest of these is truth*! Sadly, I think that we have often sacrificed the far greater experience of living our faith, hope, and love, on the altar of 'truth'.

When I first understood this emphasis in Swāmi Abhishiktānanda's spirituality I had to question my own approach to my Christian faith. As a Christian in the western Christian tradition, and particularly as a theologian, I have so often retreated into reason and intellect, in the hope that somehow orthodoxy would deepen my faith! This pursuit can be likened to a person studying biology and human anatomy in the hope of finding companionship and love.

I have come to believe that our greatest possible chance for understanding, and living, in the truth of God is through experience of the God who is truth. The expression of that truth must always be secondary to the experience of it.

The inward quest

Since Abhishiktānanda had come to believe that the Reality behind human consciousness (*ātman*) is the same as the Ultimate Reality (*brahman*), the movement within one's self, into one's own consciousness, is a move into the Ultimate Reality. This is a very basic description of the Hindu concept of *advaita* (non-duality). In other words, there is no radical duality between the source of all life, and life itself. This does not mean that the source of life, and life, are a monism. There is some measure of distinction between the two realities, yet at the same time they are not fundamentally different from one another. Abhishiktānanda's experiential spirituality emphasised this fact, and this movement towards realising the non-duality of all of the cosmos, strongly. The inward quest was essential to Abhishiktānanda's spiritual journey (see Abhishiktānanda 1989:c.4 as an example).

Abhishiktānanda did not base this notion exclusively on the Hindu concept of *advaita* (non-duality), but also on the mystery that is found in the Christian doctrine of the person of Christ. He writes,

> According to the Scriptures Christ's return in glory will bring about the summing up of all things in God ... this is also true of each one of us as regards our individual history and our unique personality. Each one of us is a microcosm and in him the whole world is recapitulated. In each conscious being who passes into God the world comes into fulfilment. (Abhishiktānanda 1989:45).

Thus, for Abhishiktānanda, just as Christ is the one in whom all things are fulfilled (Ephesians 1:10), so too each human person is a microcosm of all reality and creation, and in each person the whole of the world is or brought together, or 'recapitulated' to use the conceptual language of Ephesians 1:10 (1989:45). This was a remarkable theological insight. It stresses a number of important theological considerations.

First, it shows that one need not look outside of oneself to things that are 'other' than the self in order to find fulfilment, or even to find God, the Absolute. All of creation is to be realised and experienced through the inner life. This aspect of his spirituality was influenced profoundly by the teachings of Sri Ramana Maharshi (which will be dealt with in greater detail below). Through the practice of *ātmavichāra* (that is, asking the question 'who am I?' - *ko'ham*), one begins a pursuit to discover the self (*ātman*) that is one with the True Self (*brahman*) of all creation (Abhishiktānanda 1990:33-34). This is the discovery that fulfilment is within the self, and not outside of the self, or in someone or something else.

The second insight that can be gleaned from this theological concept is that the whole of reality is contained within each individual. This notion is not as far fetched as it may seem to the western mind which has been subtly schooled in the dualism of Newtonian science and Cartesian philosophy. The work of the physicist David Bohm points to the truth contained in this statement (for a much more detailed description of this please refer to my detailed discussion of it in Forster 2007:36-51). Even though Bohm's work was done independently, and with a scientific aim in mind, it is remarkable how his scientific discoveries correlate with Abhishiktānanda's spiritual discoveries (which had taken place at least a decade earlier than Bohm's work). Bohm spoke of a concept called the 'holomovement' named the 'implicate and explicate orders' in some sections (Bohm 1980:c.7). The central idea of Bohm's hypothesis is explained as follows:

> [T]he ultimate nature of physical reality is not a collection of separate objects (as it appears to be), but rather it is an undivided whole ... each part of physical reality contains information about the whole. Thus in some sense, every part of the universe "contains" the entire universe... (Keepin 1993:34).

I believe, that the above can be very closely related to the experience of *advaita* in the spirituality of Abhishiktānanda, that is, a discovery of the True Self, the realisation that the *ātman* (the individual self) is not separate from the *brahman* (the Absolute or Ultimate Reality that is the true foundation and source of all that exists). It is this experience, or realisation, that is the goal and aim of Abhishiktānanda's advaitin spirituality. According to him, this was the central teaching of the Upanishads.

> Upanishadic formulations have no other function than to lead to an experience. This experience is not prayer, meditation or contemplation in the commonly accepted

sense. It is a kind of consciousness, an awareness . . .
(Abhishiktānanda 1984:105).

Thus, experience of the Ultimate is a notable characteristic of
Abhishiktānanda's theology. This is based on what Abhishiktānanda
regards as the central principle contained in the Upanishads, that is,
advaita or non-duality of being, as well as a central teaching of the
Christian faith (as expressed in such passages as Colossians 1:16-17
and Ephesians 1:10). This experience takes place within the Self, and
is thus 'achieved,' so to speak, through the inward spiritual quest.

I have often been challenged on this point of view my some more
conservative Christians. Most commonly the uneasiness with this
understanding of reality comes from those who believe it to be some
form of 'new age' teaching. This cannot be further from the truth! This
is not a 'new age' teaching in any sense. It is entirely in keeping with
the scriptural view that all of God's creation comes solely from God
who is its source. More than that, all of creation gets its continued life
and is sustained by God who is the source of all that lives. It is a
mistake to think that God only 'speaks' creation into being and then
simply steps back and watches it fall apart. No, the God of the Bible is
intricately and lovingly involved in giving new and ongoing life to all
of God's creation. It is entirely orthodox Christian theology to maintain
that God is both the loving and powerful creator *creatio ex nihilo*
(creating out of nothing) of all that exits, and also the sustainer *creatio
continium* (God's ongoing work of creating and recreating all of
reality). As Luke writes in Acts 17:28, "in Him we live and move and
have our being".

Sadly those Christians who have set up a false dualism between the
God who creates, and the loving power of God that sustains and fills
all creation with life, have not understood the cosmology of the Bible
adequately. Rather, they have come to accept the teachings of
Newtonian metaphysics and Cartesian philosophy over the teachings of
Christian scripture. The impact of these influential schools of thought
have sadly eroded the Biblical view that all of reality is fundamentally
infused with the power and presence of God.

What is evident in Abhishiktānanda's own spirituality was the
struggle that he encountered as he sought to 'unlearn' the dominant and
pervasive influence of this false dualism on his faith. It will take
courage, study, commitment, and a true experience of God for us to do

the same. No doubt there will be a need to study the scriptures in order to understand and confirm this notion of non-dualism between God the creator, and us, God's creation. It will also be important to consider and understand the truly valuable and insightful discoveries that have been made in the sciences in recent decades (for some further discussion on these elements, particularly as they relate to quantum physics, and micro-biology please refer to Forster 2007:36-51, and Forster 2006, Chapter 2). These discoveries in science show that what contemporary science is discovering confirms both the view of the Christian scriptures, and Abhishiktānanda's own experience of non-duality. Much more valuable than study will be the experience of God's loving and powerful presence within your life, and the lives of those around you. Once that powerful realisation of God's all pervasive and loving presence dawns upon you, you will soon come to understand just how destructive the false dualism of an outdated western scientific paradigm has been upon our spirituality.

Sannyāsa: A life of absolute renunciation

The second significant influence on Abhishiktānanda's spirituality is sannyāsa. Etymologically of the word sannyāsa is from the words sam meaning 'totally' or 'wholeheartedly,' and *nyāsa* meaning to 'lay aside', 'resign' or 'abandon' (Rajan 1989:10). In this sense the *sannyāsi* is a person who completely abandons every care, need and concern for the world, self and others, in order to attain a realisation of the Supreme Being, sometimes called 'the Absolute'.

In Hindu religious culture *sannyāsa* is the fourth stage of life, each stage is referred to as an *ashrama*. According to the Law of Manu and the subsequent tradition, *sannyāsa* should only be undertaken when a person has fulfilled his or her duty (*rsis*) to the *devas* (celestial beings), society and family, since it requires leaving all things behind in pursuit of the Absolute (Abhishiktānanda 1984:3). The person who receives *sannyāsa dikshā* (the ritual initiation into *sannyāsa*) is "expected to be free from all bonds in the world in order to be a visible witness to the transcendence of God" (Rajan 1989:23). The renunciation required by a *sannyāsi* is so thorough that it even requires leaving behind the symbols and practises of religion. Griffiths says that a *sannyāsi* is

> ... called to go beyond all religion, beyond every human
> institution, beyond every scripture or creed, till he comes to
> that which every religion and scripture and ritual signifies
> but can never name ... *the Sannyasi* is one who is called to
> go beyond all religion and seek that ultimate goal.
> (1982:43).

Abhishiktānanda chose this life of renunciation, as a *sannyāsi*, in the knowledge that it would be the best means to attain *brahmavidya*, that is, true consciousness of *brahman*.

This concept of complete renunciation is not merely an ascetic practice, it has a far deeper theological significance, particularly in relation to the spirituality of Abhishiktānanda. The essential 'rule' of *sannyāsa*, according to Abhishiktānanda, is to be free from desire for the things of the outer world. That is, one is free from the desires of the manifest world which is seen as *maya* (illusion), or as a product of *avidya* (ignorance). The *sannyāsi* only has one true desire, that is, realisation of true and complete God-consciousness (Abhishiktānanda 1984:5).

> His [the *sannyāsi's*] desire for God is the desire for the One
> who is beyond all forms, for communion with the One -
> without – second ... With this unique and transcendent
> desire the sannyāsi may equally be called a-*kāma*, free from
> desire, and *āpta-kāma*, one whose desire is satisfied ... for
> his desire is for the Self alone, and the Self is ever-present in
> all fullness... (Abhishiktānanda 1984:5).

To be a *sannyāsi* is more a way of being than a way of living. For Abhishiktānanda being a *sannyāsi* was the embodiment of the teaching of Sri Ramana. It is a life of transcendence; a life of moving beyond, and a life of moving deeper inward, beyond the outward rituals and symbols, the names and forms (*namarupa*), and deeper inward to the Real Self.

At the beginning of the *sannyāsa dikshā* (initiation into *sannyāsa*) the initiate repeats the mantra: '*OM bhūr bhuva svah samnyastam maya*' (roughly translated as, 'all the worlds are renounced by me') (Abhishiktānanda 1984:33-34).

Accordingly, it is not only the world that is renounced, but renunciation itself:

...so long as there remains a 'by me' (mayā) in the one who
is renouncing the world, he has not yet renounced anything
at all! The mayā (I, me) is annihilated... (Abhishiktānanda
1984:34).

In the spirituality of Abhishiktānanda, absolute renunciation
(*sannyāsa*) is a central practice, that is, it renounces all attempts to
understand the Mystery of God by reliance on imperfect material
reality. It is total liberation (*moksha*), total freedom to discover the
Absolute that is both transcendent (*brahman*) and immanent (*ātman*).
Through *sannyāsa* one comes to a realisation that the true 'Self' is both
greater than, and within, your very being.

In the true spirit of *sannyāsa*, Abhishiktānanda affirmed that the
person on the quest for the absolute must renounce *sannyāsa*, or
renunciation, itself to ultimately attain *brahmavidya*. Thus for
Abhishiktānanda true *sannyāsa* was not just about renouncing outward
symbols and signs, rather it was a complete breaking down of the ego
(I, or me). As seen in the quote above, the only genuine renunciation
according to him was total renunciation, that is renouncing
renunciation itself.

Accordingly, it is only when this renunciation is complete that one
could experience something that is beyond the I / Thou dichotomy,
beyond the *tattvamasi / ahambrahmāsi* (That art thou - I am brahman)
(1984:34). This is the experience of *advaita* or non-duality.

This aspect of Abhishiktānanda's spirituality is particularly
significant for the modern world, a world that is so preoccupied with
proofs, science, quantifiable, measurable, and testable realities. It
affirms the truth that is central to the Christian faith, that the God who
created all things is above all signs and symbols; God is far greater
than creation. However, at the same time it maintains that the same
God who is sovereign and transcendent is also within all creation,
within every individual person.

In the blazing light of ... glory our very I, however personal
it may be, finds it difficult to hold itself apart from this
infinitude. Far beyond the limits to which it is restricted by
the senses or by intellectual understanding, it seems to be
extended throughout the universe through all creation, as
much outwardly beyond all things as inwardly beyond self. It
seems to reach the most inward centre of every being;

> nothing in all creation any longer appears to it as 'other', any
> more than any of God's works can appear 'other' to him ...
> [We realise] that God is everywhere and in all things, and
> that in the end God alone IS. (Abhishiktānanda 1989:44-45).

The realisation that I am not ontologically separate from God, from
other people, and from creation is of profound theological significance.
It forces the person to accept responsibility not only for their own life,
but for the lives of others. It fosters respect for other people and for
God's creation. If I exploit my brother or sister, myself or creation, am
I not ultimately exploiting God? In my mind this is one of the most
significant elements of Abhishiktānanda's advaitin spirituality. This
will be discussed in greater detail below (see particularly the sections
on science and eco-human well-being).

Advaita: Non-duality in the spirituality of Abhishiktānanda

The concept of *advaita* is absolutely fundamental to Abhishiktānanda's
spirituality. Without a clear grasp of this concept on will not be able to
hold together the complexity and depth of his discovery of the mystery
of God. So, in order to understand Abhishiktānanda's spirituality, and
the theology that flows from it, one must first understand what he
meant when thinking, speaking, and writing of *advaita*. This is what
we shall move on to consider below.

The roots of Abhishiktānanda's concept of *advaita*: Sri Ramana Maharshi and Sri Gnānānanda

Abhishiktānanda's first real contact with the concept of *advaita* came
after visiting the *asram* of Sri Ramana Maharshi and spending
extended periods in silence on the Holy Mountain (Arunāchala). It was
Sri Ramana's teaching of the knowledge of Self, the *brahmavidyā* and
ātmanamvidyā of the Upanishads that profoundly influenced the
spirituality his as he embarked on the inward quest.

Sri Ramana revealed by his example a concept of non-duality of
Self, that was based on the philosophy of Shankara[10]. Central to this

___
10 Adi Shankara (possibly 788 – 820 CE, but see below), also known as Śankara
Bhagavatpādācārya ("the teacher at the feet of God"), and Ādi Śankarācārya

concept, as mentioned above, is experience. Grant makes it clear that this teaching was not a teaching about a philosophy of being, but rather "a way of salvation through knowledge" (1991:28). Edwards describes this stage of Abhishiktānanda's spiritual 'awakening' as follows:

> The effect of Sri Ramana and his teaching, consolidated by the numinous silence of the mountain, was a qualitative shift in Abhishiktānanda's consciousness and in his sense of self-identity. This was not a change brought about by himself on his own awareness ... [it was] awakening through a *guru* who, by definition, communicates "experience" "by grace." (1997:8).

It is the guru who has reached *advaita* who communicates his or her experience of this reality to the disciple. The method that Sri Ramana taught was one of self inquiry. The purpose of this constant self inquiry was to move ever deeper into one's own consciousness, penetrating to the place where one's self-identity "the 'I' and all of created reality contingently come into being from the uncreated source beyond and beneath all the *namarupa* ... of created reality" (Edwards 1997:10).

It was Sri Ramana's teaching of this experience and the time spent in silence on the mountain that began to convince Abhishiktānanda of the value of *advaita*. Edwards notes that even though Abhishiktānanda had this overwhelming experience of *advaita* at an early stage of his life in India, the experience was only fully integrated over a long

---

("the first Shankaracharya in his lineage") was the first philosopher to consolidate the doctrine of Advaita Vedanta, a sub-school of Vedanta. His teachings are based on the unity of the soul and Brahman, in which Brahman is viewed as without attributes. In the Smārta tradition, Adi Shankara is regarded as an incarnation of Shiva.

Adi Shankara toured India with the purpose of propagating his teachings through discourses and debates with other philosophers. He founded four mathas ("monasteries") which played a key role in the historical development, revival and spread of post-Buddhist Hinduism and Advaita Vedanta. Adi Shankara was the founder of the Dashanami monastic order and the Shanmata tradition of worship.

His works in Sanskrit, all of which are extant today, concern themselves with establishing the doctrine of Advaita (Sanskrit: "Non-dualism"). Adi Shankara quotes extensively from the Upanishads and other Hindu scriptures in forming his teachings. He also includes arguments against opposing schools of thought like Samkhya and Buddhism in his works.

period of time, and that full integration only truly took place at Abhishiktānanda's death (1997:11).

From the above, it is essential to note the importance of the guru-disciple (*guru-shishya*) relationship. Thus, as Vattakuzhy notes, Abhishiktānanda's meeting with his guru (Sri Gnānānanda) from 1955 onward cemented the importance of the *advaitic* experience in his spirituality (1981:79). Abhishiktānanda describes the *guru-shishya* relationship within the context of *advaita* in the following manner:

> The guru and disciple form a couple, a pair of which the two elements attract one another and adhere to one another. As with the two poles they exist in relationship to one another... A pair on the road to unity... A non-dual reciprocity in the final realization... (1974:29).

One might liken this relationship to the relationship that exists in Judaism between a Rabbi and his students, or in Christianity between a mature and deeply spiritual Christian, and his or her disciple. However, it is essential to note that the *guru-shishya* relationship goes one step further than the above-mentioned examples, in that the guru and the disciple share not only an emotional and a rational bond, they also share a common, non-dual, experience of the mystery of God.

We shall now move on to examine the notion of *advaitic* experience that was so influential in the formulation of Swāmi Abhishiktānanda's spirituality.

The development of Swāmi Abhishiktānanda's advaitic experience

It has already been mentioned that Abhishiktānanda's experience of *advaita* was integrated in increasing measure over an extended period of time. Previous sections have suggested, however, that after his heart-attack in 1973 he reached a place where it can be said of him:

> The pilgrim to the "Further Shore" had reached his goal, his whole being was now harmonized, unified at peace; entirely faithful to Christ his *Sadguru* and wholly immersed in the depths of his soul... His Christian experience and the Upanhishadic experience had flowed back to their unique Origin. (Baumer-Despeigne 1983:329).

In essence, Abhishiktānanda could be considered a Christian advaitin – he had fully integrated non-duality into his Christian experience. According to Vattakuzhy, Abhishiktānanda did not feel that *advaita*, with its central emphasis on non-duality, posed any threat to the Christian faith (1981:109). In fact, Abhishiktānanda maintained that the advaitic experience had the opposite effect. It moves the Christian to penetrate deeper into the mystery of the Trinity. As we have already seen, the doctrine and mystery of the Trinity was of central importance in Abhishiktānanda's spirituality. He writes, "the Trinity is an experience, not a *theologoumenon*[11]... The Trinity is the ultimate mystery of the Self" (Abhishiktānanda in Edwards 1997:24). It is only in the experience of *advaita* that one discovers that the soul and God are not two (i.e., they are not ontologically separated). Abhishiktānanda understood *advaita* as pure the experience of God, beyond all notions and categories; beyond all names and forms.

In the experience of *advaita* the *advaitin* loses his or her "is-ness" (*istichheit* [German]) in the "is-ness" of the Absolute. Of course this notion is not foreign to the notion of identity expressed so clearly in the Christian scriptures. Namely, that a person's true identity is always more fully realised when the person seeks less of 'self' and more of God. This concept is perhaps most clearly expressed by Jesus himself in Matthew 16:24-25.

In this sense the 'ego' of the person is absorbed in the One True Identity. The Christian father, Meister Eckhart spoke of this journey as the journey of 'namelessness.' Vattakuzhy notes that the *true advaitin*, "... transcends every expression and every other form. He can only say 'I am' or 'I am just that'" (1981:110). Meister Eckhart conveyed a similar notion from an earlier Christian perspective, saying:

> The eye wherein I see God is the same eye wherein God sees me: my eye and God's eye are one eye, one vision, one knowing, one love (in Vattakuzhy 1981:110).

---

11 This phrase is a technical term used by theologians to refer to something that is a likely, or plausible, opinion. What Abhishiktānanda is saying here, however, is that the Trinity is not just a theological construct – a plausible opinion. Rather, the mystery of God's being, as experienced in the Triune God, is a true reality that has marked and real consequences for all of reality. Naturally that includes the human 'self' in relation to the 'Self' of God from whom all creation has its being.

Toward the end of his life Abhishiktānanda said that there is "only one vision and one visionary ... [in] that essence" (in Vattakuzhy 1981:110). That is, in *advaita*:

> Nothing remains which could help us discover any possible distinction.... Here is only the unlimited sea of Being, Sat, and a shoreless ocean of Light, a Brightness of which all things - men and devas to begin with - are simply manifestations in time and space, nāma-rūpa, names and forms. But That, Tat, is in itself without and duality, advaita. Of it nothing can be said, no definition can be given, no proper sign formulated. It is absolute Peace and Bliss, śānti, ānanda. None remains to say anything of any other, to say HE. No possible exchange even of I and THOU, only an Infinite I, AHAM, present to himself alone, aware of himself alone, the Ego Sum of Exodus, but here not heard from another, simply welling up from the inner most recesses of one's own heart. (Abhishiktānanda in Vattakuzhy 1981:111).

The experience of the advaitin, in this sense, is very similar to what L'Ange calls an "autotheistic" experience (unpublished:1). Such autotheistic experiences are characteristic of mystics and they imply that "the mystic has lost track of the distinction between God and the soul, an experience that the Flemish mystic John Ruusbroec describes as 'union without distinction.'" (L'Ange unpublished:1). This is an experience beyond the descriptive attempts of words and concepts. It is a true realization of the Absolute – a true realisation of the God outside of whom nothing can exist. This is a subtle, but very important, theological concept that is seldom considered in popular Christian theology. Orthodox Christian theology maintains, rightly, that nothing can exist 'outside' of God. If something existed outside of God then there would be a reality other than God, which is simply not possible. God is not only the creative source from which all life comes. God is also the ongoing re-creative source that sustains and maintains all living things. Creation does not exist outside of God. This does not, of course, mean that creation is the same as God. Creator and creation are distinct realities with creation deriving its life, meaning, and purpose, from the creator. However, this distinction does not mean that there is an ontological separation between the God who creates and the creation that God creates. In summary, there is no duality (*dvaita*) between God and God's creation.

In the light of this it is worth noting that in Abhishiktānanda's advaitic spirituality, some form of distinction remained between God and God's creation. Abhishiktānanda maintained that within the unity of being there is diversity of identity and substance (see the next section and the section on the Trinity for greater clarity in this regard).

It is in *advaita* that Abhishiktānanda's spirituality comes together with its clearest focuss on the mystery of the God in whom everything that exists finds its true life and meaning. It is in this non-duality, discovered through the elements of experience, the discipline of renunciation, and the quest for the discovery of the True Self (that is, the Self of all reality) that one comes to see the emphasis of his spiritual quest. These different components or characteristics all come together to form the central notion of advaitic experience in the spirituality and theology of Abhishiktānanda.

Duality and non-duality maintaining diversity without distinction

The discovery of true Self in *advaita* comes about in the discovery that my Self (*ātman*) is not 'other' from the Self of God (*brahman*). Thus, this spiritual path is not about a denial of one's individual attributes, as if one forgets who one is. Neither is it a fundamental lack of identification with these necessary attributes (Bruteau 1994:307). Rather, as one places one's identity more fully in the greater, mysterious, and more complex, loving identity of God, one comes to realize more truly who one is. One no longer identifies simply with the small "I" of one's ego. Rather, one gains true identity in the Big "I" of the Absolute Self of God, what Hindu religion calls the *brahman*.

The question that may be asked here is, "Does this not lead to Monism[12]?" Is everything not swallowed up in the one True Reality? The answer to these questions can be found in looking at the meaning of the word *advaita*. An accurate translation of the word advaita does not mean '**one**' (as in monism – i.e., there is no other but the **one**). Rather, it is more accurate to translate it **not two** (i.e., the emphasis is

---

12 Monism is the metaphysical and theological view that everything that exists is ultimate 'one'. In other words there are no fundamental divisions, and a unified set of laws underlie all of nature.

upon a lack of division, and lack of duality, rather than on an implosion of diversity into a single unity) (cf. Abhishiktānanda 1990:44).

It is a mystical union between the many that overcomes false duality between them. In other words, *advaita* is a 'unity in distinction'. Abhishiktānanda maintained that the experience of *advaita* can be likened to the unity, and distinction, of the Christian doctrine of the Trinity (cf. Bruteau 1994:310). In this doctrine there is absolute unity between the three persons of the Godhead since they share a single divine nature. However, this unity is not at the expense of the diversity and identity of each of the three persons of the Trinity. All three persons are distinct and unique, yet their distinctiveness does not separate them. The same applies in to the advaitic experience, that is, there is distinction between the self and the other, but this distinction does not imply a separation.

Christological development in Abhishiktānanda's spirituality

A discussion of Christian spirituality would not be complete without looking at the understanding of Christ reflected in the spirituality concerned. The doctrine of Christ is a central consideration in any sincerely Christian spirituality. In Abhishiktānanda's spirituality, there is a discernible struggle with the traditional emphasis in the doctrine of Christ, as expressed by many contemporary Christians, and his growing experience of the mystical Christ that encountered in India.

In an overview of Abhishiktānanda's spiritual development, one is able to discern quite clearly a change in his Christological views from the more conventional (orthodox) views of Christ to much more mystical experiences of the person, work, and will of Jesus (orthopraxy).

We shall now move on to trace the theological and spiritual development of Abhishiktānanda's Christology. This growth and change is significant, since it impacts on Abhishiktānanda's relation to conventional Christian faith, its adherents, its symbols, and its beliefs. At the same time it reflects his understanding of the Christian faith, and the person of Christ, in relation to other living faiths and their practices, with Hinduism being a particularly significant point of reference.

The 'conventional' Christian roots of Abhishiktānanda's spirituality

The first stage of Abhishiktānanda's Christological formulation and development takes place before his departure for India – this stage could be characterised as one in which his Christology was influenced by conventional understandings of the person and work of Christ. In fact the roots of his Christology can be found, as is quite common, in his own upbringing and cultural history. As mentioned earlier in the book, Abhishiktānanda was of French decent, and his parents were devout Roman Catholics (Stuart 1989:1). Naturally his upbringing would have a profound effect on his early theological formation. His Catholic upbringing led to his understanding of Christ as both the historical person - Jesus of Nazareth, and Jesus as the second person of the Trinity - Jesus Christ, Son of God.

What is remarkable about Abhishiktānanda's understanding of Christ, is that throughout his spiritual development, his doctrinal confession of Christ as Son of God remains essentially the same. However, what does change radically as his spirituality develops is his relation to, or more precisely his relationship *with*, the person of Christ. This change is particularly evident with regards to Jesus as the *logos*, or second person of the Trinity.

This first stage of his spiritual development could be characterised as a stage of devotion to the person of Christ. During his life as a monk in France he was surrounded by symbols of devotion to Christ (crucifixes, paintings and Christian writings). These were intended to evoke devotion to the person of Jesus who lived as a human, and died upon the cross and rose to life again. Dom le Saux spent time in the traditional Benedictine disciplines of prayer and reading. As a monk, his life was essentially devoted to the person of Christ in every facet. St Benedict himself expected that Benedictine monks would make devotion to Christ a central emphasis in their spirituality. St Benedict said, "Let Christ be the chain that binds you" (in de Waal 1996:1).

In Hinduism this type of devotion would be called *bhakti*. *Bhakti* is characterised by "precise modes of worship ... [and] reference to God by particular names, and certain theological or philosophical emphases" (de Gruchy & Prozesky 1991:71). Thus the Hindu lifestyle of the bhakta is very closely related to the Benedictine lifestyle of devotion.

Le Saux affirmed the central Christian belief in Jesus Christ as God, as the second person of the Trinity, and the as the incarnate logos (word of God). This affirmation of Christ's deity is done in at this stage, primarily through his life of monastic devotion to the person of Christ. After his introduction to Hindu spirituality, there is however a shift. A marked change begins influence his spirituality, in that he recognises that the 'specific' symbols, names, and images of Christ are inadequate to fully express who this mysterious person is. And so, a struggle began to emerge between his traditional devotion to Christ through symbols, and his emerging devotion to the mysterious Christ who is beyond mere symbolic comprehension.

Hindu spirituality and absorption into the divine: jnana-marga

In the early stages of his life, as is discussed above, Dom le Saux's relation to Jesus is particularly to Jesus as a person of history. Whilst elements of this understanding would change with time, he maintained throughout his life that the incarnation of Christ was an essential element of his overall Christology (1990:56). In fact, it was this very emphasis that allowed him to make some distinction between Jesus and the Hindu understandings of incarnation. He affirmed that the incarnation of Christ as a person with a particular history and context is what sets Jesus apart from the Hindu *avatāras* (incarnations) (1990:56).

In Hinduism historical events are relatively unimportant in the larger scheme of religious events; the avatāras enter the world at different times in history, but the importance of their entry into history is not to alter history itself. Their sole purpose is "to help the devotee press deeper into the mystery" (Abhishiktānanda 1990:56). Similarly, the particular form that the *avatār* takes on is merely a symbolic representation that points towards a greater mystery. With regards to the historical nature of the incarnation of Christ, however, Abhishiktānanda notes that it is important for Christians that the incarnation of Christ could only take place once. Moreover the incarnation has concrete and real effects on the history of the cosmos.

Jesus enters into the world at one particular place in history (what the Bible refers to as the *kairos* time – the right time). For Abhishiktānanda, as for traditional Christian theology, the incarnation of God in Christ is part of the evolution of human spirituality. Once Jesus had been incarnation a further step in the evolution and unfolding of God's plan for the world had taken place. History, for the Christian, is clearly moving toward an 'end' point (the Bible refers to this 'end', or goal, as the *telos* in some places and in others as the *eschaton*).

For the Christian the incarnation is thus a further revelation of the mystery of God.

> God is essentially love - so Jesus has revealed him, and he is the supreme embodiment of that Love - and Love is bound by no law. The *logos* which underlies all things is none other than the Word full of grace and truth, proceeding from the Father… (Abhishiktānanda 1990:57).

This conventional understanding of the incarnate Christ remained a part of his spirituality throughout his life, in the sense that he never rejected it as 'false', although it did loose its prominence as his spirituality grew and deepened. This shift took place as he was exposed more acutely to the mystery of God as discovered through the approaches of Hindu mysticism. He began to realise that the incarnation has many more subtle and sophisticated consequences and truths that could not be contained only in one moment of history, or one symbolic revelation of the mysterious God.

Since Hinduism placed very little stress on the importance of physical reality, in fact in most cases viewing physical reality as *maya*, (a mere illusion), the aspect of the historical Christ began to feature less prominently in the spirituality of Abhishiktānanda. He began to focus more on Christ as the 'primordial person,' that is, the *purusha* of Hinduism. He writes that, "The historical Christ is only one fourth of his mystery…" (Journal 24.4.72 in Vattakuzhy 1981:187). This quote shows that he believed that the historical Christ had a clear significance, but that there was much greater insight and discovery to be made beyond 'history.' The reason for this assertion is that it is easier to associate the transcendent Christ, who is in truth without name and form, with the mystery of Ultimate Reality, than it is to associate the transcendent God with a man from Nazareth who has a very definite physical form and historical context.

Of course the 'definite' aspect of the incarnation is what is so attractive to many Christians – particularly those who need to be able to relate to the God whom they serve. Being able to love a Lord who has suffered hunger, fatigue, pain, rejection etc., offers a great deal of comfort. Moreover, one of the central emphases of the incarnation is the understanding that Jesus, as a fully human person, was able to overcome sin and death, and in so doing has won the right to offer his life as a perfect sacrifice for our imperfect lives. This and many other elements could be listed as valuable and important elements of the 'groundedness' that the incarnation offers to us, real human persons.

However, it is also true to note that the very particular historical and physical element of the incarnation also presents some problems for many people. For example, in contemporary African Christian churches it is often quite difficult for the African believer to identify with the experience, culture, and context of a person who lived in a foreign land some 2000 years ago. That is not to mention the struggles over the centuries on issues of gender – if God chooses to incarnate God's self in the form of a human male does that have any ontological significance for 'maleness', or conversely, what does it have to say about 'femaleness'? Many of the debates around woman in the Priesthood have sadly drawn on such historical and concrete elements to oppress and marginalise women.

For Abhishiktānanda however, the move beyond the particular historical context of Jesus, and the specific form of his person, brought a great sense of discovery. He could relate to this same Christ in a myriad of creative and fresh ways.

Abhishiktānanda believed that it is the *logos* who underlies all things (cf. Colossians 1:16-17), and that *logos* is Jesus the Christ (Abhishiktānanda 1990:57). The shift that has taken place in this stage of his spirituality is subtle, but significant. What has happened is that the point of departure for relating to the person of Christ has changed from the historical person (essentially devotion to Christ through history, symbols, and doctrines) to the mysterious person (an experience of Christ as the reality that underlies all things, past, present, and futre). In this regard Abhishiktānanda said,

Christianity ... has ... burst the shackles of the Greek
anankē, the law of necessity that seemed to govern the world
and even its Creator. It has taught man that being is an even
more ultimate mystery than necessity, and that God is
beyond all that can be discovered or comprehended of him
by human reason. Man can never limit him to the truths that
he affirms... (1990:57).

Thus, there is evidence of a clear shift from reason to experience, from
doctrinal affirmation and historical evidence about the person of
Christ, to experience and absorption into the very person of Christ.
This move allowed him to associate Christ (as mystery) with the
purusha or Primordial Man of Hinduism (1990:60).

As stated earlier, Abhishiktānanda's spirituality emphasises
experience very strongly. For this reason he entered into *advaita* with
the belief that if "the Christian mystery is true, it will reappear intact on
the other side of the non-dualistic experience" (in Baumer-Despeigne
1983:314). In this stage of his spiritual development, Abhishiktānanda
moved beyond the accepted Christological affirmations, the names,
forms and symbols associated with Christ in history and doctrine. It is
not that he rejected these, but merely that he passed beyond them. In a
sense he moved into what the Hindus describe as *jnana-marga*, the
way of contemplation (or more closely translated a "renunciation of
action") (de Gruchy & Prozesky 1991:63). His quest was not to
discover the truth about Christ, i.e., the correct doctrines and beliefs
about him, but to discover the Absolute, that is Christ. One could say
that his search was for Ultimate Truth, if that Ultimate Truth happened
to be Christ then so be it. However, he was no longer bound by
traditional affirmations concerning the person of Christ to mediate his
experience of God. He had moved beyond the devotion (*bhakti*) that
had characterised his earlier Christological affirmations. He now
sought to be immersed in a spiritual experience of the divine, that is,
jnana-marga.

Abhishiktānanda's Christology in this period was furthermore
enriched by his life as a *sannyāsi*. He emphasised that the teaching of
Jesus, particularly passages such as Luke 9:58; Mark 10:21; Luke 9:62;
14:26; 9:3, advocated a life of total renunciation (1984:50). The most
vivid symbol employed by the Church that signifies Christ's own
sacrifice and self renunciation is to be found in the Eucharist.

> Indeed, in Christian understanding the Eucharist is that
> unique sacrifice (*yajña*) which Christ, the *Satpurusa*, the
> True man, the *Barnasha* or Son of Man, once and for all
> (*ephapax*) in the fullness of time offered to God as the
> summing up of all the sacrifices and offerings made by men
> throughout all ages under countless different signs and
> symbols... The perfect sacrifice of Christ the *Satpurusha* is
> the total surrender of himself beyond all signs...
> (Abhishiktānanda 1984:51).

A further significant impact on the Christology of Abhishiktānanda is
the notion of the *guru-shishya* (guru/disciple relationship). For him
Christ is always the *sadguru* (the Real Guru), whilst human gurus are
kāraka (instrumental gurus) (Vattakuzhy 1981:185). Thus, the human
gurus are only images of the one true guru, they appear in human form
to awaken the disciple to the true Guru, Jesus (Abhishiktānanda
1974:109-110). Accordingly, like the other titles of Jesus, namely,
Messiah, Son of God and Saviour, Abhishiktānanda maintained that
'Guru' is an appropriate title for Jesus. It is testified to by his being, his
method, and his message, as communicated in the Gospels (Vattakuzhy
1981:185). Jesus revealed the supreme mysteries of God which
otherwise would never have been able to be discovered e.g. the image
of the invisible God (John 14:9).

A Hindu guru teaches on the transpersonal plane, he teaches by
silence, and by communicating his experience of the Absolute to his
disciples. This is how Jesus communicated the Father to his disciples,
and even more so today, how he communicates God to us. It is
essentially a communication of being, beyond all words and forms.

> I have often written that Jesus is my Sad-guru. It is through
> his mystery that I have discovered God and myself, that I
> have caught hold of my identity. But will not the day come
> when the Guru is so transparent as to disappear in his Father
> and in his brothers...? In his first coming Jesus disappears
> for the coming of the Spirit, in his second coming he will
> disappear with all the mystery of the Father. The historical
> Christ is only one fourth of his mystery... (Journal 24.4.72
> in Vattakuzhy 1981:187).

For our purposes it is commendable to note that Abhishiktānanda had
enough courage to reach beyond what was conventional and safe in
order to find the ultimate truth of God. It is essential that we remember,

and understand, that his movement beyond conventional Christology does not mean that he rejects it, but rather that he builds upon it to move from belief concerning Christ to a deep and real experience of Jesus.

A return to the source of all life, truth, and reality – the rediscovery of the mystery of the Trinity

The final stage of his Christological development takes place during the last days of his life. By entering into the mystery of God Abhishiktānanda discovers that Christ, as a person in the Trinity, is *the* true mystery of all reality (1990:170).

His own advaitic experience of God as Trinity helps him to understand more clearly the structure of all of the rest of reality that finds its true perspective and meaning in relation to the God who creates and sustains it. His experience that the Trinity "is the ultimate mystery of the Self" (Abhishiktānanda in Edwards 1997:24) is vital to understanding Abhishiktānanda's spirituality. It is a realisation that translates from the life in the Godhead, to the life of the disciple, in other words, just as Jesus is distinct from the Father and the Spirit, yet is not separated from them, so too with the human Self of the disciple, there is distinction, but not separation. There is in a sense a realisation that a return to the non-dual Source of all contains as part of its mystery a 'matrix of duality.' That is, the mystery of the Trinity (and Christ as a person in the Trinity) is the mystery of all reality, that mystery is expressed in the seeming contradiction that is unity in differentiation.

It is only when Abhishiktānanda faces death that he can come to this very important realisation. In the first stage of his spirituality Abhishiktānanda is devoted to Christ in the symbolic and historical sense; later he realises that he needs to move beyond these symbols of devotion and seeks to do so by means of renunciation (*sannyāsa*). However, it is only when his life is to be taken from him that he realises that he can let go of his struggle to *discover* truth and simply *be*, or live, in the presence of the one who is the ultimate Truth. In a sense this is a parallel to the total renunciation (*sannyāsa*) that Abhishiktānanda saw as taking place in the death of Christ.

> The perfect sacrifice of Christ the *Satpurusha* is the total
> surrender of himself beyond all signs, as he hands over to
> God and to men the total oblation of his *sariram*[13].
> (Abhishiktānanda 1984:51)

In the weeks before his death Abhishiktānanda makes the ultimate
renunciation, the renunciation of his body, and his mental faculties.
This marks the renunciation of the struggle between religions,
particularly as he experienced it in his personal struggle between
Hinduism and Christianity. It is just before the end of his life that he is
truly able to give himself (as Christ did) wholly over to the will of
God, to be absorbed fully into the Absolute, the mystery of Being (*sat*),
Knowledge of Being (*cit*) and the Bliss of that Knowledge (*ānanda*).
The significance of the Hindu term *saccidānanda*, as it relates to the
doctrine of the Trinity, will be considered in the next section. What
needs to be noted at this point is that Abhishiktānanda saw experienced
his total renunciation as a movement of being fully absorbed into the
mystery of the non-dual life of the Trinity.

Vattakuzhy summarises Abhishiktānanda's Christology in saying
the following about Christian *sannyāsa*.

> A Christian *sannyāsi* awakened to Christ realizes the truth of
> his existence and the reality of his life as one with Christ and
> his brothers in an all-embracing love of the Father. When he
> is awakened and possessed by the Spirit, he abandons
> everything and takes refuge at the feet of the Master... The
> person has lost himself ... in the enchanting call of Christ to
> be his own. He realizes that he belongs to Christ totally, and
> that Christ wishes to share with him everything that he has
> and that he is. Then he feels at the centre of his heart that he
> came from God and has to return to the same Father, the
> source of everything ... Jesus has made him [the *sannyāsi*] a
> partner in the disclosure of his divine mystery. (Vattakuzhy
> 1981:123, see also Abhishiktānanda 1990:117).

---

13 The term *sariram* refers to the whole of the human body, including all its
mental faculties.

Saccidānanda: The mystery of the Trinity in vedantic spirituality

The concept of *advaita* has the possibility of posing a great threat to more traditional, and conservative, Christians. One of the main reasons for this is the Christian belief that God is absolutely transcendent, that is, God is radically different from, and distinct from, God's creation – of course there is a measure of truth in such assertions. In truth God is 'wholly other.' The creator must have some measure of distinction in order to be the one who creates – this distinction allows once to tell the difference between the creator and the creators creation. However, the overemphasis upon distinction in traditional western Christian theology has often led to a radical duality between spirit and matter, and most particularly a false duality between God the creator and God's creation. As a result of this overemphasis of distinction, and in some cases even separation between Creator and creation, some Christians have come to question how a spirituality of non-duality, such as that of Abhishiktānanda with its central emphasis on *advaita*, can be true? The answer, as we shall see, is to be found in the mystery of the Trinity.

Abhishiktānanda understood that the mystery of the Trinity could be given a fresh perspective that would allow some forgotten elements to be brought to the fore again, and create a more holistic understanding of the mystery of God, by the expressing this mystery with the word *saccidānanda*.

This word is made up of three separate root words, *sat*, meaning 'Being', *cit*, that means Knowledge, and *ānanda*, which means Bliss. For the Hindu the experience of *saccidānanda* means a true Knowledge (*cit*) of True being (*sat*) that brings about an experience bliss, i.e., an experience of "true joy and peace, complete felicity." This blissful state is called *saccidānanda* (Abhishiktānanda 1990:170). He further describes this experience by saying,

> I am for ever established in my own centre, in the very centre of all things, in the *ānanda* of *cit* and *sat*, in the perfect bliss of Being and of Being's awareness of itself (Abhishiktānanda 1990:170).

For Abhishiktānanda, the terms *sat*, *cit* and *ānanda* aid the Christian to find a fresh pathway and understanding that will guide his or her movement into the mystery of the Trinity.

In *sat* the person adores the Father, the first person of the Trinity. The Father is the unoriginated Source of all that exists; Being itself (that is *nirguna brahman*, or God without attributes). The Son, is the Knowledge (*logos*) of the Father. "*Cit* is the presence to itself, the consciousness of itself, the opening to itself, of *sat*" (Abhishiktānanda 1990:179). The Father expresses himself in the Son in whom he communicates his very Being, yet at the same time he is distinct from the Son (the Son is *saguna brahman*, or God with attributes). Thus they are not one in the sense of a monism, each has a distinct identity. Nonetheless, there is no duality between the Father and Son, there is only advaitic (non-dual) relationship. Hence, one does not simply say that the Father and the Son are 'one'. Rather, one comes to realise that they exist in a complex and subtle relationship of unity with one another best expressed in the assertion that they are 'not two'. It is at the very heart of this non-duality that there is *ānanda* or Bliss. This is a bless that stems from full self realisation and true individual identity (the identity of a loving Father and a loving Son) who at the same time have an ontological unity that stems from their defining relationship.

In traditional Christian theology this would be spoke of as the co-inherence, or mutual indwelling, of the Father in the Son, and the Son in the Father, in a relationship of non-duality that is Bliss - *ānanda* (Abhishiktānanda 1990:185). It is in this sense that Abhishiktānanda says, "the Trinity is an experience, not a *theologoumenon*... The Trinity is the ultimate mystery of the Self" (Abhishiktānanda in Edwards 1997:24).

In discovering the mystery of the Trinity, which is both the source and the substance of the true advaitic experience, the advaitin realises that he or she is also taken up into the mystery of love that is the Trinity. There is no duality, yet even within this lack of duality, one does not loose one's true identity. In fact, one's true identity, the true Self, can only be truly discovered in the One True Self. The realisation that my Self (*ātman*) is not other than the True Self (*brahman*), is the central teaching of the doctrine of *advaita* and the experience of *saccidānanda*.

Thus, it is hoped that in understanding that distinction does not need to lead to division, that the mystery of the Christian doctrine of the Trinity will be enriched, not only in terms of it gaining a fresh vocabulary to express the mystery of the Trinitarian life, but more particularly that it will enrich the spiritual seeker's intimate engagement with the God whose very life is a life of Bliss. The spiritual pilgrim can thus come to discover that true life (both spiritual and physical) comes from the source of truth life (the Father) and can be experienced in a relationship with a God who is tangible and identifiable (the Son), and that this will bring the Bliss of true identity and life in God (through the Spirit that brings life). Clearly there is a great deal of value in this approach, not the least of which is that such an expression, and experience, of the Trinity can correct the error of duality that has crept into contemporary western theologies of the Trinity.

Conclusion

As we delved more intentionally into the theology that supports the spirituality of Abhishiktānanda, we have outlined the major theological strands and characteristics that informed his quest for an authentic experience of God that would not only be shaped by traditional understandings of, and approaches to, the Person of Christ. This process has shown that his spirituality was primarily informed and shaped by mystical experience. Furthermore we considered how his life as a *sannyāsi*, with the particular emphasis upon renunciation that is so central to that concept, was very influential in the formation of his understanding of *advaita* (non-duality).

While my own spiritual quest has been rooted firmly within what could be considered traditional Christian theology and spirituality, I was deeply challenged by Abhishiktānanda's integrity to move beyond the elements of culture, and even religion, in order to truly experience the joy and bliss of being in Christ. His spirituality has challenged me to reconsider the words and concepts that I employ in speaking of God, and my experience of God. I am challenged to consider whether my experience of the true God shapes my theology, or whether I have fallen into the trap of allowing mere symbols, phrases, and concepts, to shape my experience of God. I have come to agree that God is beyond mere human language and philosophy, and that there is need, at times, to chart a new course towards the same unchanging God for the sake of spiritual renewal, rediscovery of truth that has been lost or forgotten, and the discovery of unknown truths that will turn up along the way.

What remains now is to ask what contributions Abhishiktānanda's spirituality and theology have to offer for both the theologian and the sincere spiritual seeker.

Abhishiktānanda's contribution to contemporary Christian spirituality and theology

Understanding the groundbreaking and novel approach to Christianity that arises out of Abhishiktānanda's spirituality, one comes to realise that it has a great deal to offer towars the renewal Christian spirituality, and the further development of Christian theology and faithful discipleship. His spirituality was pioneering, it was a discovery brought about by much struggle and searching – truly one could say that Abhishiktānanda worked out his "salvation with fear and trembling" (Philippians 2:12). In our contemporary Christian context where there is such great sensitivity to syncretism and shallow adaptations of ancient and diverse spiritual traditions, it is necessary to outline carefully what contributions he has made to Christian spirituality and theology, so as to avoid misunderstanding and unnecessary critique.

If one honestly, and openly, considers such positive contributions, it will facilitate an awareness of areas where growth is possible, both for the enlightenment of the Christian disciple, and for further discovery of the mystery of God's self.

Standing on the shoulders of those who have gone before

Perhaps one of the greatest contributions that Abhishiktānanda has given to the study and practice of spirituality and theology is his own experience of God. In an age that often seems to be dominated by scientific reason and empirical discovery, we must not discount the value of spiritual discoveries! Whereas some persons journey to the depths of the world's oceans, or venture into 'outer space' to discover things about our universe, Abhishiktānanda could rightly be considered an explorer and a pioneer. His discoveries are, however, not made in 'outer space,' but in the sacred 'inner space' of the spirit.

As has been mentioned a number of times in this book, Abhishiktānanda endured great inner and outer turmoil in the discovery and development of his spirituality – in this sense his spirituality can truly be called a 'quest.' His struggle is a great gift to generations of scholars, practitioners, and theologians, of spirituality, since it means that those who have come after Abhishiktānanda can learn from his struggle and discoveries. The intense struggle that he endured need not be repeated by others, and the discoveries that he made can be integrated (and transcended).

The author wonders how much richer the spirituality of Abhishiktānanda would have been had he been able to make the discovery of 'simply being' much earlier in his journey? As we note above this was a discovery that only came at the very end of his life. Unfortunately that question can not be conclusively answered.

Perhaps it is the struggle itself that makes Abhishiktānanda's spirituality so appealing to many who sincerely search not only for religious truth, but for a true experience of God? Perhaps it is because he was so human, so imperfect, and so honest, that his spirituality is so real for many sincere seekers of such truth? What is certain however is that Abhishiktānanda's spirituality was pioneering work. It displays courage, integrity, and forms a worthy example to other pilgrims who will take 'uncharted' courses in their spiritual journey. In terms of the courage exemplified in his struggle, it is essential that those who look upon his life and work never forget the time and context in which he lived. Abhishiktānanda was active in interfaith encounter, in seeking the truth in faiths other than Christianity, some 30 years before the Second Vatican Council that began in 1964. Why is this significant?

Prior to 1964 the official attitude of Churches in general, and the Catholic Church in particular, was less than favourable toward other faiths. The First Vatican Council (December 1869 - July 1870) had marked the beginning of an extremely conservative and oppressive era in the Roman Catholic Church. Among other things, it declared that salvation was only able to take place within the Catholic Church (*extra ecclesiam nulla salus* [Latin]) (cf. Pillay & Hofmeyer 1991:219-220). The consequence of this is that many devout Christians did not even consider the possibility that God could work in any other Christian denomination, let alone any other living faith! It is in the light of this that the significance of Abhishiktānanda's move to India is accentuated. Although there had been a number of prominent Catholics in India before Abhishiktānanda, such as Robert De Nobili the 17th century missionary, none had every come to India with the express purpose of forming a contemplative centre along Benedictine and

Indian cultural and religious lines. Those who had come before had most often sought to convert the local populace to the Christian faith, rather than seeking to live with, and learn from, those whom they encountered.

The Second Vatican Council ushered in an attitude in the church that was far more favourable to religions other than Christianity. The Council regarded other religions as 'positive,' clearly affirming the possibility of salvation and revelation in other faiths (cf. Gaybba 1981:90; Hick & Hebblethwaite 1988:80-86). Even though Jesus Christ was seen as the "constitutive cause of salvation" in other religions, the council had affirmed the value and richness of other faiths (Knitter 1985:128).

Some readers who uninitiated in the theology of inter-religious encounter may find this suggestion somewhat alarming! I have often been confronted by sincere Christians in this regard. The questions are most often framed along the lines of the uniqueness of Jesus Christ as God's chosen pathway, or means, of salvation. For example, "doesn't the Bible (New Testament) say that one cannot be saved by anyone other than Jesus (Acts 4:12)?", and "doesn't the Bible (New Testament) affirm that Jesus is the only way, the only truth, and the only way to the Father (John 14:6)?" Indeed, these are valid questions! Many Christians have been perplexed by such questions throughout the centuries. The second Vatican Council did not dispute the unique salvific efficacy of Jesus. Indeed, if one studies their statement one would see that they affirm that wherever there is salvation it is through Jesus. However, they made the significant step of affirming that one is not saved by any one religions *expression of Jesus*. We must bear in mind that the Christian religion, and all Churches, religious structures, symbols, and the associated theology, as human constructs. We created these 'religious vehicles' in order to manage our faith in relation to God. These things are not salvation in themselves, rather they are the pointers, aids, guidelines, that lead us more closely to the one who saves, namely Jesus Christ.

Thus the second Vatican Council affirmed the reality that God is not bound by religious expression. God could be active in all of history and in a variety of cultural and religious expressions. What was certain, however, was that wherever persons were saved, and sin was dealt with (either personally or structurally) God was working through the person of Jesus Christ. In order to make this statement they had to affirm that sometimes Jesus would operate 'anonymously' in a religion or culture. In other words, one may be able to recognise the work of Jesus without it having to be expressed in the same historical and contextual guise as the Christian expression of Christ's person and work.

This point deals very creatively with questions about God's love, mercy, grace, and justice, in relation to history. What does this mean? Well, if one could only be saved through the action of Jesus at a particular moment in history (for example the death and resurrection of Christ in the early first century) then all persons who lived before that would not have access to salvation. If God committed such persons to hell God could be considered unjust (since such persons did not have the opportunity to choose for or against salvation in Jesus Christ). However, orthodox Christian theology has come to understand that the cross is the central act of salvation in Jesus Christ. Yet, it has two equally important elements to contribute. First, we would say that Jesus death and resurrection are 'constitutive' of salvation. Traditional Christian soteriology maintains that we are saved by those acts – in his death Jesus pays the price for our sin, and in his resurrection he overcomes the consequence of sin, namely he overcomes death. This constitutive element is effective across all of time (both in the centuries that followed after the historical events of his death and resurrection, and in the many centuries that came before). This assertion leads to the second, and equally important, emphasis in the salvific work of Jesus on the cross. Not only is the cross of Christ 'constitutive' of our salvation, it is also 'illustrative' of God's salvific will. in the events of the death and resurrection of Jesus we are exposed to the loving, gracious, and merciful will of God to save humanity from personal and structural sin. Clearly this 'illustrative' will is not bound either by historical time or specific cultural and symbolic events. The fact that God wishes to save all persons is an aspect of God's loving will.

It must be noted that this understand cannot be confused either with religious pluralism (which affirms that there are many individually valid and different paths to salvation in various religions), or universalism that suggests that all persons will automatically, and ultimately, be saved. This view, often referred to as the view of the 'anonymous Christ' emphasises the unique and efficacious salvific activity of Christ that requires a specific human response in order to deal with personal and structural sin.

Of course this view is entirely in keeping with what the New Testament teaches. Many Christians are not aware that there are various accounts of 'non-Christian' persons who are saved from their sin. In the symbolic language of the Biblical writers salvation is most commonly expressed in terms of entry into 'heaven'. Perhaps the two clearest examples are to be found in the Gospels. First, there is the account of the Transfiguration of Jesus where one reads of Elijah and Moses and their encounter with Jesus (Matthew 17:1-9). Both of these men were prophets of the Jewish faith who had died centuries earlier. A second, and perhaps clearer account, is the rich man and Lazarus (Luke 16:19-31). In this account we read of the father of the Jewish nation, Abraham, in heaven. Some have argued that Abraham, Moses, and Elijah could have been saved by their adherence to the laws of the Jewish faith. This is not only unlikely, but highly implausible when one considers the stringency of these laws. However, a more compelling argument against that notion is the argument for Islam. If one is saying that a person who is in the line of the Semitic faiths (Judaism, Christianity, and Islam) could be saved by adherence to the law alone then one has to do away with the New Testament teachings that speak of the law being powerless to save because of human sin (cf. Romans 8:3). No, it would be more sensible to accept that God has been active in Christ, saving persons in various contexts and times by his gracious will. This will is most clearly expressed, and is fundamentally constituted, in the saving death and ressurection of Jesus on the cross.

The consequence of the deliberations of the second Vatican Council on other living faiths meant that interest in, and co-operation with, other faiths was far more acceptable and common.

However, there is no doubt that persons such as Abhishiktānanda where pioneers in this area long before the official policy of the Church had accepted interfaith encounter and mutual enrichment from other faiths. Abhishiktānanda's active engagement with Hindus, learning from them and being enriched by their faith and spirituality, no doubt had a significant effect on later moves within the Church.

Thus, when one considers how Abhishiktānanda contributed to Christian theology and spirituality in this regard one will see that he was the first Christian monk to fully adopt the life of *sannyāsa*. He was the first to realise that "fidelity to Christ and the advaitic experience could co-exist" (Rajan 1989:92). There is no doubt that those who followed after him had learned a great deal from Abhishiktānanda. Most notable of these is Dom Bede Griffiths who took over Shantivanam ashram after Abhishiktānanda left for his hermitage in the Himalayas in 1968. Fr Bede refers to Abhishiktānanda as a pioneer "in the attempt to adapt monastic life in India to the traditional forms of Indian life and prayer," and as someone who "showed the most profound insight into the relation of the Hindu to the Christian tradition" (Griffiths 1982:23, also see Forster 2007).

The scholar, and the practitioner of spirituality, can benefit a great deal from studying and emulating the central elements of the spirituality of Abhishiktānanda. The nature of his spirituality, as both Hindu (or more specifically advaitin) and Christian, makes it particularly significant for those who seek to use spirituality as a means of inter-religious encounter. One of the complexities of inter-religious dialogue is that is hampered by the language and philosophy that constitute the conversation. Very often when one seeks to engage doctrinally between different faiths one can fall into the trap of trying to compare 'apples and pears.' Shared encounter and experience is a much more valuable platform upon which to build sincere and rigourous engagement. A common experience can be much more powerful than any doctrinal construct. Certainly, doctrine is a necessary outworking, or product, of experience. But doctrine should follow experience, and not the other way around.

The Christian should be more able to deal with the struggle of passing beyond the names and symbols of Christianity in quest for the Absolute, with the sure knowledge that many have passed this way before and found the mystery of the triune God intact on the other side. In a sense the spiritual practitioner or scholar is able to pick up where Abhishiktānanda has left off. He or she is able to pass through the struggle and insecurity of the unknown with a greater sense of comfort because of the discoveries that were made by Abhishiktānanda during his life's journey. There is no doubt that Abhishiktānanda was a pioneer in this field. However, with this comes a realisation that what he began in his life can be taken further by those who follow. It is in this sense that we can stand on the shoulders of Abhishiktānanda. He was a pioneer that embarked on a journey of discovery, and has left his discoveries as a foundation upon which we can build.

Spirituality as a meeting point for inter-religious encounter

Another of the fundamental contributions made by Abhishiktānanda is to the practice of interfaith encounter. The first thing that needs to be noted in this regard is the respect with which Abhishiktānanda approached the Hindu faith. It seems clear, not only from Abhishiktānanda's writings, but also from his life and actions, that he sought to learn from, and be enriched by, the practises and beliefs of the Hindu people. It would be wise for those Christians in the 'global South', in places such as Africa, India, and Latin America, to learn some lessons from this approach. Increasingly the negative and destructive effects of 18th and 19th century European and American missionaries are being exposed. There is a real desire among, for example, African Christians to strip the faith that they inherited from its colonial roots and rediscover the richness and depth that can come to bear upon Christianity from African tradition and religion.

Whilst Christianity in its present form has innumerable strengths it also has some weaknesses. Perhaps foremost amongst these is that it has, to a great extent, lost sight of the value of spiritual discipline and the depth of spiritual experience. A great tragedy in the Christian Church has been the dissipation of the contemplative and intuitive disciplines associated with the experience and practice of spirituality. Abhishiktānanda realised that reason without experience is dead; doctrinal affirmation and outward devotion do not lead one to living the fullness of what the Christian faith is, and has to offer. Hence, he began to look toward the riches contained in the spiritual practices of the East attempting to adapt them for use in his Christian faith. Perhaps the finest examples of this adaptation are, living as a Hindu monk (*sannyāsi*) and his immersion in the example of Sri Ramana's experience of *advaita* as a motivation for realising the Absolute. This adaptation has the potential of greatly enriched not only the practice of spirituality in Christianity, but also has the possibility for a much wider influence as will be seen in the section discussing Social and Ecological responsibility. Ewert Cousins affirms the value of spiritual experience, not only as it benefits the faith of the community, but also as a source of theological reflection.

> In a basic way, spirituality is experiential; it is bound up with praxis, specifically orthopraxis. As such, it should provide material for theological reflection. At the same time spirituality should be enriched and guided by theology. (Cousins 1992:58).

Moreover, it is not only the Christian faith that stands to benefited from Abhishiktānanda's adaptation of the spiritual practice of the East. As mentioned above Christianity has both strengths and weaknesses, the same can be said of any faith, and in this context it can be said of Hinduism. Whilst Hinduism (particularly in the form of the Vedantic schools) has a strong contemplative base, it often falls short in the area of social and ecological responsibility, when measured against global ecological standards. This may have its roots in the belief that physical reality is unimportant and is only an illusion (*mayā*).

In the East the Christian faith is often regarded as inferior because of its lack of contemplative spirituality. However, spiritual practitioners, such as Abhishiktānanda and Bede Griffiths, as well as theologians in the same line, such as Raimundo Pannikar, have done a lot to give the Christian faith the opportunity for much greater spiritual credibility in the East. A strength of Christianity is that it is a historical faith, in other words, it is grounded in history. The outworking of God's plan in history is evidenced in the world around us, that is, God's plan for salvation is both a spiritual and a historical reality. Thus if Christianity were to gain greater credibility in the East, it has the possibility of bringing a balance between the overly spiritual and the overly materialistic. This could no doubt foster far greater sense of urgency for social and ecological concerns in the East, and spiritual concerns in the West.

On the same topic, Abhishiktānanda's spirituality is of tremendous significance for inter-religious encounter in that it is practical and experiential in nature. One of the greatest criticisms levelled at those involved in inter-religious dialogue is the fact that they engage in debate about theological and philosophical concepts that are often irreconcilable, that is, often they are trying to compare apples with pears with very little success.

As was previously suggested, the problem with dialogue is that it is dependent upon language. Language in turn is dependent upon representative symbols and philosophical constructs to communicate deeply complex realities. On the other hand, in the practice of spirituality, persons often experience the same or similar things (as in the case of Christian monks and Hindu *jnāni*) (cf. Cousins 1992:55-59). This common experience can serve as a basis for mutual respect and a common starting point to begin dialogue, and more importantly encounter, with each other and each other's faith traditions. Such common experience leads to mutual discovery and enrichment. The realisation that "dialogue at the level of spirituality in coming to know and understand people of other faiths as people of prayer and spiritual practice, as seekers and pilgrims with us..." can be invaluable in fostering a sense of mutual respect and trust, that is essential for any form of encounter (Arai & Ariarajah 1989:2).

Along with this comes a second realisation that, "In walking with the other, with the stranger, like the disciples on the road to Emmaus, we have had, in our sharing, the experience of recognition. We have seen the unexpected Christ and been renewed" (Arai & Ariarajah 1989:2).

Psychological and scientific significance

Traditionally the life of a *sannyāsi* is a life of *purnam* (perfection or fullness) (cf. Vattakuzhy 1981:113). It is a life of integration, a life of communion; a life in perfect relation with God and with all of God's creation. Abhishiktānanda's spirituality has unity (or non-duality, *advaita*) as its central and shaping tennet. There is no 'other' of which to be afraid, no other that can threaten the self, there is no duality (*dvaita*) only *advaita* (non-duality).

This is not only a very healthy spirituality, since it is fundamentally true at an ontological level, but it is also a very healthy psychology and seems to align itself with developments in contemporary human and natural science. In this regard Abhishiktānanda's spirituality resonates strongly with the position of, for instance, the transpersonal theorist Ken Wilber and that of many quantum theorists[14]. Central to Wilber's

---

14 For a detailed discussion of Ken Wilber's integral theory, and recent developments thereof in relation to Bede Griffiths theology, and psychology as

views of reality is what he calls the "Spectrum of Consciousness" (1975:107).

> At the heart of ... the "Spectrum of Consciousness" ... lies
> the insight that human personality is a multi-levelled
> manifestation or expression of a single Consciousness...
> More specifically, the Spectrum of Consciousness is a
> pluridimensional approach to man's identity ... which ranges
> from the Supreme Identity of cosmic consciousness through
> several gradations or bands to the drastically narrowed sense
> of identity associated with egoic consciousness (Wilber
> 1975:106, please refer to the diagram at the end of Appendix
> A for a visual representation).

The aim of Abhishiktānanda's spirituality is *advaita* (or non-duality).
This is essentially a conscious realisation or experience, an experience
that my self is no other than the True Self. As this quote from
Abhishiktānanda, which has been used numerous times in this book,
illustrates: "the Trinity is an experience, not a *theologoumenon*... The
Trinity is the ultimate mystery of the Self" (in Edwards 1997:24). This
realisation equates with the transpersonal level in Wilber's spectrum of
consciousness. The transpersonal level is a level of consciousness
beyond the personal, one could call it a 'cosmic consciousness'. There
is no longer any real, ontological, separation or duality between the
self-identity of the individual (*ātman*) and the One True Identity
(*brahman*).

> On this level, man [sic] is identified with the universe, the
> All - or rather, he is the All ... this level is not an abnormal
> state of consciousness, nor even an altered state of
> consciousness, but rather the only real state of
> consciousness, all others being essentially illusions... In
> short, man's innermost consciousness ... is identical to the
> ultimate reality of the universe. (Wilber 1975:107-108)

A second area on which the psychology of Ken Wilber and the
spirituality of Abhishiktānanda agree is what Wilber calls "unity
consciousness" (Wilber 1979:141). This is the consciousness that is
associated with the level 'Mind' on Wilber's spectrum. I believe that
this is what Abhishiktānanda experienced in *advaita*, that is, complete
unity with all existence. Abhishiktānanda and Wilber both agree that

---

a discipline, please see Forster 2006 and Forster 2007.

this unity of consciousness "is entirely present now" (Wilber 1979:141; see Abhishiktānanda 1984:51). Hence, there is no 'way' to arrive at the Unity (*advaita*) that already is; it is more a matter of becoming conscious of the reality that is non-dual. Spiritual discipline is not a striving to create non-dual unity, rather it is an exercise in coming to realise the truth that already exists.

As mentioned above, Abhishiktānanda's spirituality also seems to justify and corroborate many discoveries and hypotheses in natural science. The implications of discoveries in quantum theory seem to testify to the fact that all of reality (all of creation) is not disconnected, but is in fact completely interconnected. Such discoveries and interpretation of them affirm that creation, rather than being a large mechanism, as was the view of Isaac Newton, could more accurately be described as an interconnected, interdependent living organism[15]. Thus, as this quote from the quantum physicist Schröedinger says:

> Inconceivable as it seems to ordinary reason, you - and all other conscious beings as such - are all in a all. Hence this life of yours you are living is not merely a piece of the entire existence, but is in a certain sense the whole... Thus you can throw yourself flat on the ground, stretched out upon Mother Earth, with the certain conviction that you are one with her and she with you. You are as firmly established, as invulnerable as she, indeed a thousand times firmer and more invulnerable (in Wilber 1975:108).

It is worth noting how this view can be related to the spirituality of Abhishiktānanda and in turn can be related to many others (such as the view of the quantum physicist David Bohm mentioned earlier in the book). There is no doubt that Abhishiktānanda's spirituality has firm foundations, not only in the riches of age old spiritual traditions, but also in the new discoveries and developments of the social and physical sciences. It is grounded in an experience of Ultimate reality, that seems to agree with developments in psychology and an emerging and growing science. In both these fields the practice and study of his spirituality can be of great value not only for research, but also for the further discovery of the very Ground of Existence.

---

15 For a detailed discussion of the Newtonian-Cartesian worldview, and the advances in natural science as a result of quantum theory, please refer to Forster 2007 and Forster 2006.

The spirituality of Abhishiktānanda, and others in this field, serves as a spiritual balance to scientific and other discoveries about existence and reality that seem to dominate western consciousness. In a sense one could say that spirituality as a science, is a means of discovery and experimentation as much as any other scientific venture would be.

Community and eco-human well-being

Perhaps two significant criticisms that could be raised against Abhishiktānanda's spirituality is that, on the surface at least, it seems to be extremely individualistic and because it is so introspective it does not really have much to offer in terms of Western notions of liberation and social action. Thus, one could ask the question: Does what seems to be an extremely introspective individualistic spirituality have anything to do with the community of the Church, and can it contribute anything towards the liberation of the oppressed and alleviation of exploitation of people and creation?

A clear answer to the above question would be 'Yes' on both counts. As far as community is concerned, it must be remembered that Abhishiktānanda was a member of a number of 'communities' in the broad sense. First, he was a Benedictine monk and a *sannyāsi*. In both of these capacities he had opportunities to share his spirituality and encourage others on their spiritual journey – his identity was shaped and informed by those he interacted with, and of course he also sought to shape and form others (cf. Baumer-Despeigne 1983:323-329).

Although one reads constantly of Abhishiktānanda's desire for solitude in order to enter into the mystery of God more deeply, there is no denying his joy, and the significance of his guru-disciple (*guru-shishya*) relationship with March Chaduc (cf. Baumer-Despeigne 1983:324-326). It is here that one sees most vividly how his spirituality contributed to the life of another. In commenting on the Mystical Communion model of the Church, Avery Dulles quotes the following:

> The result of intimate association, psychological, is a certain fusion of individualities in a common whole, so that one's very self, for many purposes at least, is the common life and purpose of the group... One lives in the feeling of the whole and finds the chief aims of his will in that feeling (Cooley in Dulles 1987:48).

This is essentially a statement of identity. Where does the individual find his or her true identity? It is only to be found in the One True Identity. Bruteau, an interpreter of the notion of *advaita* in the spirituality of Abhishiktānanda, makes a very important point about human relationships and community, as they flow from this understanding of non-duality.

> ...they [all people] are sharing in the one existence , the one consciousness, the one happiness, because all that any one is, is completely open to each one, is totally given and shared with each one. Nothing is hidden, nothing is reserved for oneself alone, nothing is refused (Bruteau 1994:312).

This leads to what was raised above as the second criticism. What of social and ecological responsibility? From the above quote, it is clear to see that the spirituality of Abhishiktānanda has an ultimate concern for all of reality, since the one who is immersed in the Self is immersed in the same Self as all of creation. In referring to social and ecological responsibility the term, *eco-human well-being*, coined by Paul Knitter in his book 'One earth, many religions: Multi-faith dialogue and global responsibility' (1995, Orbis) is appropriate.

How does an introspective spirituality relate to *eco-human well-being*? First, it gives rise to a new experience of the mystery of God, and creation. That is, the realisation that God is not separate from humanity, and that creation is central to an appropriate and responsible relationship with God since it is grounded in the fact that my Self (*ātman*) is not separate from the Self of the rest of the universe and God (*brahman*). If developed further this realisation has the possibility of giving new insight into almost all areas of Christian theology and practice. If I am not separate from the rest of creation (i.e. if there is no duality or *dvaita*), and I choose to exploit creation, am I not exploiting myself, and at an even deeper level am I not exploiting God? The same can be said for human relationships and the structure of society. In this sense the spirituality of Abhishiktānanda gives the very motive for engaging in any struggle for *eco-human well-being*. According to Gustavo Gutiérez, it is from spirituality, the

> ...rich experience of following Jesus that liberation theology emerges ... [spirituality] represents ... a deeper penetration of the very wellspring from which this kind of theological thinking flows (Gutiérez 1988:xxxii).

This quote leads us into the next section.

Spirituality as the source of theological reflection

Increasingly western theologians are asserting that reason and philosophy are not the sole, or even the primary, sources for discovering the revelation and will of God. There are an increasing number of theologians who are of the mind that spirituality serves as a valuable source for the development and furtherance of systematic theologies. Notable among such are Raimundo Pannikar and Ewert Cousins. Cousins writes about his own theological methodology that,

> In a basic way spirituality is experiential; it is bound up with praxis, specifically orthopraxis. As such it should provide material for theological reflection. At the same time spirituality should be enriched and guided by theology. In this book I am viewing spirituality as experience ... and theology as the reflection on experience (1992:59).

There is no doubt that the spiritual discoveries of Abhishiktānanda and other spiritual persons are making an impact on the sciences, social sciences and other related disciplines. These discoveries need to be articulated and investigated. They need to be put to the test in order to move ever deeper into the mysteries of existence and reality. In a world with large scale plurality of religion, philosophy, and lifestyles, the disciplines of mutual discovery are of the essential importance in fostering understanding, respect, and avoiding unnecessary confrontation and oppression that is often associated with ignorance or fear of the 'unknown other'. In this regard Cousins writes,

> The encounter of the world religions calls for the forging of a Christian systematic theology that will encompass within its horizons the religious experience of humankind (1992:77).

It is here that Abhishiktānanda, in particular, has much to offer. Long before the categories of modernism and postmodernism became popular he was attempting to 'break down the dividing walls' of culture, religion, and worldview. His spirituality is based on experience, experience can be shared and can foster points of common connection. Furthermore, his spirituality is based on the notion of *advaita*, that is, unity with the one Reality that transcends individual religions or cultures. Such common experience can foster a sense of unity and trust which can serve as a basis for working together toward greater peace and harmony amongst the people of our world.

Conclusion

This book has sought to offer some insight into the groundbreaking spirituality of Abhishiktānanda. At the start of the book I suggested that there is a dire need for fresh, creative, and brave, expressions of spirituality that will engage and enliven the lives of sincere seekers of God in Christ. It was suggested that forms of faith, and spirituality, that were inextricably bound to symbols, concepts, and language, would ultimately be discarded by those who find that there is a conflict between the symbols and concepts they hold to, and the symbols and concepts that others hold to. Of course, a sound solution to this problem is to find a spirituality that is based not upon symbols, but upon experience of the truth that the symbols and concepts seek to express and articulate.

Abhishiktānanda's spirituality is one vivid example of such a spirituality. Of course his particular context, even his methodology, may not be what is needed for every person. However, his life is a testimony to the kind of courage and devotion that is not afraid to struggle and undergo radical challenge in order to change – all this for the sake of moving beyond symbols and expressions of truth, to an experience of truth itself. Of course, this approach to the mystical life is contextual. Regardless, it is hoped that the principles and spirit of Abhishiktānanda's spiritual journey will encourage you to discover new and creative truths within your own cultural and religious context. Moreover, the theology of this remarkable journey challenges us to rethink the constructs of our faith, asking which elements are 'trappings' of our cultural heritage, and which are expressions of a true experience of the triune God's mystery in Christ.

It has been well over a decade since I first encountered Abhishiktānanda's uncommon spiritual path. A great deal has changed in my own life over the years. I too have struggled to find an authentic and sincere devotion Christ, yet my context has been that of an African Christian whose experience of Christ was shaped and framed by the colonial emphases left within the Methodist Church of Southern Africa my Methodist missionaries from Britain in the 19th century. Whereas Abhishiktānanda's journey was one of integrating East and West, mine has been one of integrating South and West. There is no doubt that the richness of African culture and religion has a great deal to offer spirituality and doctrine. Jesus, after all, is not English, he is not American, or European, Jesus is the embodiment of the tremendous mystery of the loving creator God – the God who created all persons.

My path is different, but my desire is the same. I long for a true experience of the living Christ that is not trapped in religion. I long for that experience to enliven my faith, transform and heal my community, and renew and enliven my loving devotion to Christ and service to others.

May you take great courage as you seek to follow an uncommon spiritual path to find Jesus.

Appendix: A glossary of Sanskrit terms

Sanskrit term	Explanation
acharya	teacher. Often the head of an ashram.
advaita	non-duality
aham brahmamsi	I am Brahman (God)
ananda (ānanda)	pure joy, bliss
ariti	waving of lights and incense
ashram	abode of ascetics, place of spiritual work
ashrama	stage of life, stages of the spiritual journey
atman	God within each person, Spirit
atyesthi	death ceremony
avatara	incarnation, descent
avidya	ignorance
brahmachari	moving in Brahman, a student
brahman	the Absolute, God
brahmavidya	knowledge of God
bhakti	devotion
bhakti marga	the way of devotion
chit (cit)	consciousness
darshanas	philosophies
devas	shining ones, gods

Sanskrit term	Explanation
dharma	the law of life
diksa	ceremony of initiation
dvaita	duality
grhastha	householder
jivanmukta	one who has attained liberation during his lifetime. A person who is one with God
jivatman	individual soul
jnana marga	the way of knowledge
karma	action, work
karmamarga	the way of work
lila	the play of God, God's purposeful activity in the world
mantra	prayer or sacred word
maya	creative power, magic, illusion
moksa	final liberation, salvation
murti	image or form
nirguna brahman	God without attributes
nirvana	state of liberation in Buddhism
om	the sacred syllable, symbol of Brahman, the creative word
parabrahman	the Supreme Spirit
paramatman	the Supreme Spirit
puja	sacrifice

Sanskrit term	Explanation
purnam	fullness
puranas	mythological stories
purusha	man, cosmic Man, cosmic Person, archetypal Person
purushottaman	the Supreme Person
rishis	seers
rita	the order of nature
rsis	duties associated with the asrama
sadguru	the true guru
saguna brahman	God with attributes
samadhi	the final ecstasy. Death
samsara	the wheel of life
santana dharma	eternal religion
sannyasa (samnyāsa)	renunciation
sannyasa diksha	the ritual initiation into sannyasa
sannyasi	a monk
sat	being
shakti	the power of God
shanti	peace
shantivanam	forest of peace
shiva	name of God, the destroyer and regenerator
tapas	self control, penance

Sanskrit term	Explanation
vanaprastha	forest hermit
veda	knowledge, sacred scripture
vedanta	the end of the Vedas, philosophy
vishnu	name of God, the preserver

(Based on glossaries of terms in Griffiths 1983:133-136 and Rajan 1989:275-280).

A visual representation of Ken Wilber's pluridimensional view of consciousness (discussed in Chapter 2).

Adapted from Wilber 1975.

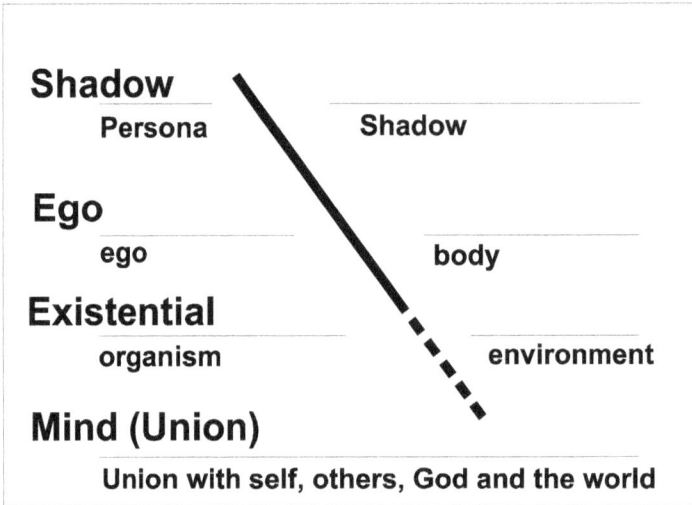

Shadow
   Persona   **Shadow**

Ego
    ego   **body**

Existential
   organism   **environment**

Mind (Union)
Union with self, others, God and the world

Select Bibliography

Abhishiktānanda 1974. Guru and disciple. (First edition 1966). London: SPCK.

Abhishiktānanda 1976. Hindu-Christian meeting point: Within the cave of the heart. (First English edition 1969, first French edition 1966). Delhi: ISPCK.

Abhishiktānanda 1984. The further shore: Three essays by Abhishiktananda. (First edition 1975). Delhi: ISPCK.

Abhishiktānanda 1989. Prayer. (First edition 1967). Delhi: ISPCK.

Abhishiktānanda 1990. Saccid□nanda: A Christian approach to advaitic experience. (First English edition 1974, first French edition 1965). Delhi: ISPCK.

Arai, T Ariarajah, W 1989. Spirituality in interfaith dialogue. New York: Orbis books.

Baumer-Despeigne, O 1983. The spiritual journey of Henri Le Saux - Abhishiktānanda. Cistercian studies 18 4, 310-329.

Bohm, D 1980. Wholeness and the implicate order. Routledge and Kegan Paul.

Bruteau, B 1994. In the cave of the heart: Silence and realization. New Blackfriars No 65, 301-318.

Bruteau, B (ed) 1996. The other half of my soul: Bede Griffiths and the Hindu - Christian dialogue. Wheaton: Quest Books.

Cousins, EH 1992. Christ of the 21 st century. Brisbane: Element.

De Gruchy, JW and Prozesky, M (edd) 1991. A Southern African guide to world religions. Cape Town: David Philip Publishers.

D'Costa, G 1993. Whose objectivity? Which neutrality? The doomed quest for a neutral vantage point from which to judge religions. Rel Stud No 29, 79 - 95.

De Waal, E 1996. Seeking God: The way of St Benedict. London: HaperCollins Publishers.

Dulles, A 1987. Models of the Church: A critical assessment of the Church in all its aspects (Second edition). Hong Kong: Gill and MacMillan.

Edgerton, F (ed) 1944. The Bhagavad Git□. New York: Harper & Row.

Edwards, F (ed) 1989. A new vision of reality. London: Collins.

Edwards, F 1997. Self identity and consciousness in Abhishiktānanda: A case study. Science and vision: Qualitative research and consciousness. 1-27 (ed. I Meulenberg-Buskes). Pretoria: HSRC.

Forster, DA 2005. Post-human Consciousness and the Evolutionary Cosmology of Pierre Teilhard de Chardin, in Grace and Truth – a journal of Catholic reflection for Southern Africa. Volume 22, No 2, August 2005, pp. 29-44.

Forster, DA 2006. Validation of individual consciousness in strong artificial intelligence: An African theological contribution. Pretoria. Doctoral Thesis. University of South Africa.

Forster, DA 2006a. Identity in relationship: The ethics of ubuntu as an answer to the impasse of individual consciousness. In The impact of knowledge systems on human development in Africa" du Toit, CW (ed) 2006. Pretoria. Research institute for Theology and Religion, University of South Africa.

Forster, DA 2007. Christ at the centre - Discovering the cosmic Christ in the spirituality of Bede Griffiths. Kempton Park. AcadSA Publishers.

Gaybba, B 1981. Vatican II's approach to non-Christian religions. Christianity among the religions. 77-105 (WS Vorster ed). Pretoria: UNISA.

Grant, S 1991. Towards an alternative theology: Confessions of a non-dualist Christian. Banglore: Asian Trading Corporation.

Griffiths, B 1982. The marriage of East and West. London: Collins.

Griffiths, B 1982. A new vision of reality. (F Edwards. ed). London: Collins.

Gutiérrez, G 1988. A theology of liberation. London: SCM Press.

Hick, J Hebblethwaite, B 1988. Christianity and other Religions: Selected readings. Philadelphia: Fortress Press.

Hick, J and Knitter, PF (edd) 1987. The myth of Christian uniqueness. London: SCM press.

Knitter, PF 1992. No other name? A critical survey of Christian attitudes toward the world religions. New York: Orbis books.

Knitter, PF 1995. One earth many religions: Multi faith dialogue & global responsibility. New York: Orbis books.

Keepin, W 1993. Lifework of David Bohm: River of truth. Revision 16.1, 32-46.

L'Ange, IN unpublished. A re-appraisal of the autotheistic experiences of the mystics. Introduction to the Study of Religion Lecture Notes. 1-17.

le Saux, H (Abhishiktānanda) 1983. The eyes of light. New Jersey: Dimension books.

Pannikar, R 1977. The Vedic experience: An anthology of the Vedas for modern man and contemporary Celebration. Pondicherry: All India Books.

Pillay, GJ and Hofmeyer, JW (edd) 1991. Perspective on Church history: An introduction for South African readers. Pretoria: HAUM Tertiary.

Rajan, J 1989. Bede Griffiths and sannyasa. Banglore: Asian Trading Corporation.

Stuart, J D M 1989. SwāmiAbhishiktānanda: His life told through his letters. Delhi: ISPCK.

Vattakuzhy, E 1981. Indian Christian sannyāsa and Swami Abhishiktānanda. Banglore: Theological Publications in India.

Vorster, WS (ed) 1981. Christianity among the religions. Pretoria: UNISA.

Wakefield, GS (ed) 1984. A dictionary ,of Christian Spirituality. London: SCM Press.

Weber, JG (ed) 1977. In quest of the Absolute: The life and work of Jules Monchanin. London: A. R. Mowbray & Co Limited.

Wilber, K 1975. Psychologia Perennis: The spectrum of consciousness. Journal of Tranpersonal Psychology 7.2,105-131.

Wilber, K 1979. No boundary: Eastern and western approaches to personal growth. California: Center Publications.

Wilber, K 1980. The Atman project: A transpersonal view of human development. London: Theosophical Publishing house.

Wilber, K (ed) 1982. The holographic paradigm and other paradoxes: Exploring the leading edge of science. London: Shambala Publishing.

www.ingramcontent.com/pod-product-compliance
Lightning Source LLC
Chambersburg PA
CBHW031603040426
42452CB00006B/396